Before SEVEN-THIRTY:
Practical Ways to Empower Yourself and Save YOUR Relationship *Before* Giving Up

Fina Oria

Foreword by Award–Winning Author,
Professor Jamela Franklin, Ed.M., M.A.

DLB 730 Press
―――――――――
Norcross, Georgia

A must read if you're dating, married, divorced, or even single!

Before SEVEN-THIRTY: Practical Ways to Empower Yourself and Save YOUR Relationship Before Giving Up can be a priceless guide to identify several relationship issues that are like kill switches. A doomed relationship is rarely a surprise to anyone. What can you do to not fall prey to a disastrous relationship? Why do you find yourself in the same types of relationships? Well, if you would pay attention, the tell-tale signs are usually present.

You will learn that the warning signs are by-products of many issues, including:

- harboring chaotic behaviors
- supporting external conditioning
- being oblivious to the warning messages

A great relationship requires a need to challenge yourself and take charge of your life. Ultimately, *the key* is not to ignore or brush off the warning signs as early as right after you've said, "Hello".

Before SEVEN-THIRTY: Practical Ways to Empower Yourself and Save YOUR Relationship Before Giving Up is more than a self-help book for individuals to resolve relationship issues before matrimony. It is a catalyst for self-empowerment and a GPS to tap into your Qi (chi) or life force by setting the bar high for inner peace and continuous self-improvement.

(©) 2018 Fina Oria

All rights reserved. No part of this book may be reproduced or transmitted in any form or by any means, electronic or mechanical, including photocopying, recording, or otherwise, without prior written permission from the publisher. For more information regarding permission to reprint materials from this book or getting discounts on bulk orders, email your request to Decodelife@before730.com.

This is a work of non-fiction, but some names have been changed for privacy purposes.

This book is not intended as a substitute for the advice of psychotherapist, psychologist, or licensed physician. It is sold with the understanding that the author is not engaged to render any type of psychological, legal, or any other kind of professional advice. The content in this book is the sole expression and opinion of its author.

Oria, Fina
Before SEVEN-THIRTY: Practical Ways to Empower Yourself and Save YOUR Relationship Before Giving Up

ISBN: 978-1-970075-00-7

Published by DLB 730 Press
P.O. Box 930261
Norcross, GA 30003
www.before730.com

Cover design: Demetri Noel-Jeune, DNJ Design
Couple's image on cover by Josethestoryteller on pixabay.com
Editor: Lisa Dawn Martinez, The Finicky Editor
Author photograph: Gabriel Desgranges

Printed in the United States of America

All quotes or references are printed with permission from authorized parties or where Fair Use apply.

This book is dedicated to my three young kings: Khyri Holder, Xaa'lin and Xa'Kaden Heru El-Bey.

CONTENTS

Foreword	i
Acknowledgments	iii
Introduction	v
Inside Nelumbo Nucifera	vii

PART I

Chapter 1	I Saw the Light	1
Chapter 2	Clean Slate: The Ideal Echelon of Self-Discovery	11
Chapter 3	Current Trend of Marriage: Quicksand	19
Chapter 4	Signs from First Year *Before SEVEN-THIRTY*	57
Chapter 5	Open Exchange: Hello!	59
Chapter 6	Behavior Speaks Volumes	67
Chapter 7	Life Regressions	85
Chapter 8	Who Needs Money?	99
Chapter 9	Criminal Minds—Sticking up Your Future!	107
Chapter 10	No Caviar	115

PART II

Chapter 11	Before the Big Hoopla	125
Chapter 12	Pastoral Counseling	133
Chapter 13	I AM Not	139
Chapter 14	Line in the Sand	145
Chapter 15	Be Realistic	151
Chapter 16	Be Flexible and Willing to Learn	155
Chapter 17	Seek Counseling to Resolve Past Issues—Critical!	161

Chapter 18	For All the Goddesses of Our Time	167
Chapter 19	For the Eros of Our Time	185
Chapter 20	Expansion of the Mind	197

PART III

Chapter 21	After "I Do"	203
Chapter 22	So, You're Still Talking?	205
Chapter 23	Be at Peace	207
Chapter 24	Grow Stronger Together	211
Chapter 25	Let Each Other Be	215
Chapter 26	Trust: Not a Light Rider	219
Chapter 27	Create Your Own Footsteps	229
Works Cited		233

FOREWORD

Before SEVEN-THIRTY: Practical Ways to Empower Yourself and Save YOUR Relationship Before Giving Up is exceptional! Fina Oria has artfully chronicled the trials and tribulations that individuals experience before, during, and after relationships, yet most dismiss. As a young woman who saw the warning signs in some of her own relationships but failed to acknowledge them, Ms. Oria decided to write a book that would assist others in recognizing and avoiding the pitfalls that she had experienced.

After reflecting upon her life, she realized that if she had acknowledged and followed the admonition of the warning signs, she would not have experienced most of the painful lessons that ensued. However, as a result of those experiences, she became more observant of her life and the lives of others. The wisdom she gained from those experiences prompted Ms. Oria to write this wonderful book.

Each chapter is written with sage wisdom, insight, and humor. Fina captivates the reader with her witty anecdotes and timeless advice. Reading this beautifully written book made me laugh, ponder, agree, and reflect. As I turned each page, I was eagerly anticipating the next tidbit of advice and the next delightful scenario. She expertly counsels the reader without judgment, which is an art. A few of the book's chapter titles "Open Exchange: Hello", "Before the Big

Hoopla", "Seek Counseling to Resolve Past Issues-Critical", and "Be at Peace" give you a glimpse into the content that awaits the reader.

Lastly, *Before SEVEN-THIRTY: Practical Ways to Empower Yourself and Save YOUR Relationship Before Giving Up* is a must read for anyone, before entering a relationship with someone else, who desires to be emotionally, spiritually, and mentally balanced, healthy, and whole.

Professor Jamela Franklin
Award-winning Author, College Professor, Holistic Life Coach

ACKNOWLEDGMENTS

WHAT A JOURNEY! There is no other way to describe the inception of this book—it was just meant to be. It certainly would be incomplete without giving dues to a few people.

A mother's undying love to my young kings, Khyri, Xaa'lin, and Xa'Kaden, who have taught me the true meaning of unconditional love! I wrote this book for you and with you in mind. I envision that the future will be one of splendor for all three of you.

My soul-traveling partner, holistic practitioner | instructor, Xaa'el Heru El-Bey, I manifested our love story through this book before we met. Thoughts and words are powerful indeed. Thank you for reminding me of what I had forgotten about people and that knowledge alone is not enough.

Much love and great appreciation to my parents, Clairzimene and Sauveur Louis, for all the sacrifices that you both have made for me and my four siblings (Ultride, Soneck, Fabienne, and Nathanael) to have a better life.

My editor, Lisa Dawn Martinez, you were a God-sent angel in disguise. Thank you for teaching me what it takes to be a better writer and having the patience to work with a new author.

Acknowledgments

I can't say enough great things about my gifted graphic designer and consultant, Demetri Noel-Jeune of DNJ Designs, who brought my vision for the book cover to life. You are exceptional!

A special thank you to Professor Jamela Franklin, Ed.M., MA, author of *Reflections of the Soul: A Memoir* and *I'm Not Crazy—Just Menopausal*, who wrote the book's Foreword, gave me my first blog radio interview, and took me under her wing.

Thank you to Christmas Miller, intuitive consultant and author of *Illuminations: A Road Less Traveled: A Modern Day Seer's Journal of the Human Experience*, who has shared valuable resources and insights to get me started on my new journey.

A long bow to Mike Loomis, author of *My Book Launch Planner: Simple Strategy and Tested Tactics for Your Book, Podcast, or Product* for guiding me to a successful launch.

I can't forget to show love to Dr. Vashonna Etienne, Afrocentric Psychotherapist, who interviewed me on her YouTube platform.

Much gratitude to my beta reader and line editor, Kit Duncan. Thank you to all my endorsers for taking the time to review my book, and everyone else who has helped with this unparalleled and incredible ride. To all the couples who permitted me to enter their private lives by sharing with me their time, experiences, and wisdom—thank you. Lastly, a warm embrace to all my readers who purchase my book. I am humbled by your support and interest in my work. I hope my words will serve you.

INTRODUCTION

BLENDED FAMILIES ARE now the norm. We've heard of the many reports that state 45-50% of first marriages will end in divorce. This high probability is causing both men and women great angst whenever they hear the word, marriage. But what if there was a way to help keep your family and marriage intact before you even walked down the aisle?

It doesn't have to come as a surprise when a marriage fails, although it frequently does. Many newlyweds, on some level, knew they might be making a mistake, even through their smiles, as they exchanged their vows.

So why didn't they act on that?

The signs that the marriage may not last were there all along, but couples seldom pay attention to them.

Those warnings are straightforward, and the issues can be solvable if recognized early enough. *Before SEVEN-THIRTY* delves into these signals coming from various compartments of a person's history: abusive issues, childhood trauma, criminal background, and financial matters. It gives couples permission to have open dialogue about previously forbidden subjects.

While the entire book is designed for both genders, it also has targeted chapters geared toward men and women specifically. The book then funnels into how the newlyweds should work on their marriage and what to do to keep the relationship strong.

This book is about more than merely observing signs during your courtship, before marriage. It's also about empowering yourself with the necessary tools to survive the trials that inevitably come with being in a relationship.

With the divorce rate so high, the institution of marriage is in serious trouble. Couples often take up to a year to plan the wedding and almost no time to plan the marriage. It is time to acknowledge the paradigm shift when it comes to how you handle yourself in your relationships. Time to open your eyes to, and open the dialogue on, the many things that will take place during your marriage, so you can not only survive but also thrive. This is my goal. I want to ring that alarm, be that wakeup call. *Before SEVEN-THIRTY*. Before you go crazy. Before it's too late.

It's heartrending to see how many families are drowning in the misery that comes with dealing with a bad breakup. So, this is my gift to you to help reduce the unnecessary stress that we put on ourselves when we try to walk before learning how to crawl. This is what some of us do before marriage, but *Before SEVEN-THIRTY* can help you slow down to do an impartial tour of your life and your relationship before you say *I do*.

INSIDE NELUMBO NUCIFERA

BIRD SONGS ECHOING in the breeze,
Vibrant colors of eternity emerge;
The wind caresses, and yes,
Dances in light rhythm.
Telepathy is the showcase of its expression;
Unity is the revelation of its recalls.
Who wants in?
Is it you?
The battered souls of Erde?

Fina Oria

PART ONE

Chapter 1

I SAW THE LIGHT

WHAT'S GOING ON in many households across the world these days is quite troubling. We live in a period of instant gratification where we expect results, like, yesterday. We forget to connect to our world, and, to top it off, we hurt each other more than any other intelligent being on this planet. We fall out of love, it seems, as quickly as we fell in love. We marry today while a divorce is lurking right outside the bedroom door the day after the honeymoon, waiting to be let in.

But do you have to welcome it?

I am a mother who believes both parents have a duty to raise their children. I think we need to go back to the drawing board as far as our relationships are concerned. We often hear about people divorcing, even when we would rather escape the pain and hear otherwise; but perhaps hearing about it gives us the opportunity to re-examine our own relationships.

I am the second of five children who grew up in a household with both parents. My parents have been together for more than 40 years, and by the look of things, only death will end their union now. My mom has been the loyal I'll-follow-you type of wife, and my dad is too tired to allow himself to go astray. Despite my parents' long union, something very important was still missing from my childhood: a formula for a happy and satisfying relationship.

Could there be a formula for something so complex?

Even as a child, deep down I believed that there was more to the unexcited life that I lived. I was always different from my siblings—very outspoken, direct, analytical, and somewhat of an overachiever. It didn't matter much what our environment was like because I was determined not to be just an extension of my parents. If their relationship consisted of anything unhealthy, I told myself that I would do the opposite. And that's what I did. My parents made their own mistakes and lived their lives. Now, I had to live mine. I couldn't continue to blame them for what they did or didn't do. Remember, our parents cannot teach us what they do not know.

So, as a young adult, I put myself through college with the help of my husband at the time. I took care of myself and took control of my life. However, life has a way of testing us when we think we've overcome all obstacles. After my husband returned from a six-month military training, I knew that something wasn't right with my marriage, but I couldn't figure out what. Despite all the disappointments from my teenage years, I was unprepared when my marriage ended after just five years.

I was a twenty-six-year-old mother with a toddler, living in a state far away from my family. I went through a deep depression for nearly a year. I was numb and confused. It took me six years to understand what was wrong. The formula for disaster was already there, even before my ex and I had exchanged our vows.

Since my divorce, I've been in a few relationships. Their lesson: Stop attracting and rescuing self-destructive men—such individuals may end up destroying my happiness and sense of peace through their unfavorable actions.

After my divorce, I went through the daily seesaw of being a divorcée. Those moments taught me that I could have more control over my life if I would just slow down and open my eyes to the signs the Universe was giving me.

Those signs can be like the falling snow, beautiful yet potentially deadly.

This is where *Before SEVEN-THIRTY* comes knocking. In numeric form, the term 730 is an expression that simply means crazy or mentally unstable. It's used as a police code to mean such. In the legal system, a defendant might file a 730 motion to get examined to certify if they're mentally fit to stand trial. I also read years ago that inmates or mental patients had to take their medicine at that time each morning. Either way, the title came to me when I was about a quarter of the way through writing the book. I thought it was fitting because I want to reach those people who want to work on their relationships. The ones who don't want to go mad because of mostly avoidable and unnecessary relationship drama. No, you don't want to be 730.

Don't lose your gifted mind or trivialize how great your married life could be if you would open your fourth eye—your view into your higher consciousness. This is your warning: you must be a godmother to your own life and become your own lighthouse by not ignoring the early courtship signs that could later destroy your marriage and your happy home.

If I've done it right (and I hope I have!), my book should accomplish at least three things:

1. Guide you to first observe and then work with the signs that the Universe shares with you early on in your relationship.
2. Help rock the boat, setting you in motion if you're in a new or existing relationship and you're confused about what you are currently experiencing.
3. Help you realize that you are the creator of your own happiness and that you don't have to keep suffering in the name of love.

Before SEVEN-THIRTY is mainly for those, young or old, who are dating. Nevertheless, the keynotes in here will touch anyone, whether newly involved, married, in a domestic partnership, or looking to be prepared when love comes knocking. These topics are universal and thus will be relatable to all. For those of you who want to get married one day, this book can propel you to eliminate some of the hardships that could later lead to divorce.

Divorce is a tough and sad decision. Breakups are painful enough, but to some people, divorcées seem to hold a comment bubble over their heads shouting, "I destroyed my family unit! I'm a failure!"

But you need not to feel that way. If you understand the universal laws, then you'll see that you just did not pay attention soon enough to know that the person you married came to your life for a reason.

Before SEVEN-THIRTY cannot guarantee to prevent divorce, but it can assist those who could have a wonderful relationship if they pledge to put in work early on.

What I'm sharing with you is what I've learned after my own divorce. Learning or knowing is one thing, but taking action is a completely different ballgame. I would be a fool to think that I have all the answers. The last laugh would definitely be on me. When it comes to matters of the heart, the wind rules. Nevertheless, deep down, I inexplicably know what I need in my life to have a great relationship. So do you. You only have to listen.

When I tell people that I've written a relationship self-help book, usually the next question that follows is, "Are you a relationship expert?" I consider myself as a relationship facilitator based on experience. My views are from riding this never-ending, invigorating yet suspenseful rollercoaster ride called *Trials of Life*. I'm still on that ride, but I'm much more conscious. I'm not a wisenheimer, nor am I perfect in all that I do. However, the messages in this book are inspired and divinely guided information. My credentials come from my own journey and those of others that have chosen to share theirs with me.

Some of you might be thinking that all the stones have been turned already. If that is true, then why is the divorce rate so high?

Clearly, there is still a need to reach out, even to those who think they have their relationships figured out.

While many like to work from without, I prefer to work my way from within. I wanted to use my own véda to help others shed the mystery associated with having a great relationship. This is not a ticket to Breakup Ville, but rather a ride to awareness and sanity. The point is to notice what's not working and what is and then do something about it, whether it's leaving X behind, which is not always easy, or signing up to work through the kinks.

I want to see people heal themselves and resolve whatever is disconcerting them. Maybe instead of a Bachelor's in Computer and Information Systems and a minor in Business Law & Public Policy, I should have gone the psychology route—it has always called to me. Regardless, the path has led me here. To you.

Any time you help another who is in distress, you have to tap into that person's psyche and work from there. I give much respect to those in the field, whether it's a psychiatrist or psychologist, life coach, or what have you because it takes much patience, discernment, and a removal of self to help troubled individuals.

I have an obsessive thirst for knowledge, which has turned me into an insatiable reader. I've been a bookworm since I was 12 years old, and I yearned to escape my reality. While presently way beyond my juvenile years, I love purchasing books, and I'm also a well-known patron at the local county library. Yes, some of us actually still go to the library!

I usually head straight to 100-299; that's the philosophy/psychology and religion/spirituality section. I'm drawn to that side by rote because I'm on a spiritual journey and have been for the last fourteen years.

It wasn't until I wrote this book that I realized, to my surprise, that I haven't been a big enthusiast of relationship self-help books. Yet for years, I've been lending an ear to friends, and sometimes even strangers, with relationship woes. I ask impartial questions that guide and open their senses in making their own decisions. I'm a natural at this. It happens so much that it almost seems like people can intuitively pick up my healing vibe.

For instance, I was in one of my favorite stores shopping for an upcoming vacation when an employee walked up to me after less than five minutes and began to ask what I thought about the guy she had recently started dating, who happened to be a relative of her ex.

"If he hasn't called me, does that mean he's not interested?" she asked with a hopeful gaze.

"Well, it depends," I answered as I looked up, somewhat taken aback by her question. "How long has it been since you called him? Could he have been busy but will get back to you later?"

She shrugged and with a sudden blank stare whispered, "I don't know."

I stopped walking and then declared, "If you find yourself always making the first move to reach out to him, then you might be onto something."

She continued to follow me in the store to talk about what was troubling her as more customers started to stroll in on that cloudy Saturday morning. When I was done shopping, I thought she wanted to talk some more, so after spending a couple of Franklins too many, I gave her my card and said she could call me.

I'm a frequent shopper at that store, so I hope to see her again, but with much more calmness, less puzzlement, and happiness in her steps.

Later that day, as I was about to tell my mom what had happened, I got a phone call. On the line was a friend from overseas, who specifically requested my "psychological assistance".

No, I don't have a Talk to Me Hotline!

I thought, how fortuitous. I was just about to tell my mom how people are drawn to me when they need an equitable person to listen to them. At that moment, a soul in need did just that—reached out to me. My heart expands at times like these.

Anyhow, I wanted to see what was out there as far as relationship advice goes, so, of course, I went to the local library. It was exhilarating as I drove home in anticipation, and I skimmed through the first four books that night to see what had been written on this fascinating subject called marriage.

What I took away from those books was that we've analyzed human relationships from under a microscope on a scientific, religious, fictitious, comedic, systematic, conventional, and reactive level. Whew, that was a mouthful! By now, you would think that we would have it all figured out.

Many of you are shaking your heads, thinking heck no, we're not even close! Since I'm a maverick, I would also like you to break away from that run-of-the-mill and mechanical thinking, just for a moment. I want you to start tackling your relationship from a more proactive and clean-slate approach. It's good to revert to the beginning when it feels like you just can't get it right. Don't wait for the worst to happen to you and your partner before you make adjustments.

Universally, it means using the time during your courtship wisely. If you waste it now, trust that, in retrospect, you will regret what you missed.

Welcome to Fina's world, a compilation of some of the relationship doom signs that I've gathered during the dismal yet liberating "Aha!" moments of my darkest hours, and those of my many friends and acquaintances. Buckle up because, if you're extra judgmental and only semi-conscious, you may inadvertently wake up by the end of this crossing. Take a dive past RBS (Relationship BS) into Created Nirvana with me.

Chapter 2

CLEAN SLATE: THE IDEAL ECHELON OF SELF-DISCOVERY

THE SKY IS blanketed with nimbostratus clouds. A breezy wind picks up to a gale, and the trees sway violently in all directions. Raindrops start to dance on the ground like water in a heated pan while deafening thunder and blinding lightning strike every five seconds.

The weather is trying to tell us something. This is nature's caveat. If you're somewhere unsafe, you'd better take cover—and fast.

Have you ever noticed that some type of natural foreboding precedes most disasters, whether we detect it pre- or post-event? I'm convinced that nature does the same in our relationships. Just as you pay attention to the weather, you should be on the watch for signs from your partner, especially while you're dating.

As humans, we think that we know what we're doing without needing a little help from Mother Nature. Don't assume that she works through the environment and yet passes you by. You're also a part of Mother Nature, and she has great power over you. Yet, knowing that she'll have her time to teach you better, she ignores your disrespect. As the Queen of Symbology, she talks to you through signs and warnings. She knows it is so painful when *The One* who is supposed to love you bruises your heart instead.

The signs could tell you if you're with someone who complements and balances you. They can also show you if this person is noxious like a deadly fume that might obscure your bright future. Once you're clued in, you can decide what to do.

This can be explained in terms of life's experiences. Someone once asked me if I believe in love. It took a few seconds to roll the dice in my head before I answered that yes, I sincerely do. But love in its purest state is how we experience it as a child before we are aware. As an adult, after we've been conditioned and try to find ourselves and our purpose in this crazy world, love can be byzantine. How many of us could honestly say that we haven't taken a sip from that proverbial cup?

I'm not about to preach about love. I can't teach you how to love without you having the experience. However, I can coach and guide you on how to treat yourself and how to deal with certain of your self-destructive or neurotic issues as well as those that storm in from the partner you bring into your life—your potential husband or wife of bliss or of doom. It's a matter of proactively acknowledging and parenting one thing: The imminent signs.

Many of us make the serious mistake of not acknowledging them early enough when we're dating. We get angry and confused when things start to fall apart in our marriage, yet it is our own disobedience to the lessons of life that brought us here. Unlike many people, I deal with the signs, because I know that they are there for a purpose. The few times that I ignored them, I paid a hefty price. I've made many mistakes when I didn't understand the warning signs during my courtship, so now I'm careful to open myself to them. I take heed when the same issues continually pop up in my life. I stop whatever it is that I am doing, think about what is not working, and talk to my partner to figure out a solution.

It's not an easy task, but it can be done. *Before SEVEN-THIRTY* is a good precipitator, but the real work starts with you accepting the challenge to stop continuing down the road of doom.

Your relationship is a work of art, a unique beauty that requires you to notice the little things that make it what it is. But you'll only see it as such when you take the time to admire its intricacies and step back to see the whole masterpiece, not just one stroke, with faults and all.

Before SEVEN-THIRTY was born out of my desire to shake the trend, even if to a few, and share how to have peace of mind before and after experiencing heartache from those who claim to love you so much. It is also about how to take ownership of your relationship by hitting the brakes before you go crazy.

We live in a challenging time when a relationship is not as simple as it could be due to the changes of our time. We are usually on the go. Work-life balance is in short supply. We are rewarded for spending more time at work and less time with the family. We have more external distractions such as the Web with its instantaneous barrage of news, social networking, and the ever-increasing subjective information feed on television and in magazines. We are getting more educated but less connected with the fundamentals of a simple life.

You must put things in perspective, or you will simply be trying to find your way on a stormy voyage without a compass. The work begins with that first eye contact. If you want a great marriage, you must be ready to work through the early signs of destruction while dating. Our experiences are not as singular as we think. You can make a difference in your own life by saying to yourself right now, "I will stop the madness *Before SEVEN-THIRTY.*"

Are you in wholeheartedly?

If you're already married but see some of the discussed signs in your relationship, you can still galvanize and mend what's not working. It's not too late to improve. Of course, it would have made your life much easier if these issues were addressed before marriage, but you have a second chance. Kudos to you for wanting to make things better! You will feel the immediate difference in your relationship once the problems that have been destroying your union are acknowledged and you work together to resolve them.

However, the struggles and taxing days of being with someone who does more damage than good can challenge us to the core. This is when we need to stop and assess.

Hindsight is a tormenting teaser and our greatest teacher. It's like our personal Library of Congress, where we can learn from our past and use that information for a better and brighter present and future. My ex-husband's now-deceased grandmother, with whom I had a wonderful relationship until it took an unexpected turn, tried to warn me, but she didn't express it in a way for me to truly understand. Since I'm older now, I'm making the best of my enlightenment and experiences.

I'm not trying to convert anyone to the ways of *my* heart and consciousness. The effects of our life experiences are relative, because two people rarely feel relationship pains the same way at the same time, even when they're both hurting. But we can empathize with each other. There's not a one-size-fits-all solution. We all face our own problems in our own relationships, and sometimes even similar problems require alternate solutions. The most important thing is to understand the problem and then resolve it.

You don't always need to search a little blue book to find the underlying cause of an issue. Believe it or not, most of the time you already have the answers. It requires you to reduce the distractions, pay attention, and listen to the messages that come to you. Do not underestimate the knowledge that you have within you, especially when it comes to solving the problems you face in your relationship.

What would you do if you were alone, with only yourself to rely on?

Imagine yourself in a big cage with a lion, a tiger, or a venomous snake. I have no doubt that, even though you may lose in the end, you will suddenly embody such strength and determination that you will be ready to fight until your last breath. You're not about to let an animal, no matter how ferocious, come at you as if you're a dead leaf.

It's no different when it comes to resolving your relationship qualms. You will face all types of challenges in your relationship. However, it is up to you how you tackle them. You can let those challenges deplete your sanity and strength, or you can look at them as gifts to move forward with confidence.

Our views can vary on what makes a relationship great, but during my interviews, I discovered many common threads from couples who I consider to be in healthy and loving partnerships. They adore each other. They listen to each other. They work together to build their future. They eliminate external distractions and work through their problems. But most importantly, they do not allow the media or other people to define their relationship. Both the husbands and wives are at peace with self. They have learned to close the outside door when necessary for the betterment of their relationship.

So, go deep inside yourself. Shut off all distractions, including quieting your busy mind. Learn to trust what comes from within. Believe that you know more than you think you know.

I frequently must remind myself, and even my older son, of this internal wisdom.

Case in point: At 7:56 we were on our way to the last day of school when my (then younger) son turned to me and asked, "Mommy, does RJ have more money than you?"

"I don't know," I replied.

"Well, I think he does because he always has cash, but you never do. Well, sometimes you do," he continued.

"He may have more cash in his pocket, but I have more in the bank. But that's not the most important thing. What's the most important thing?" I tested him.

"God," he answered.

"And," I nudged him on.

"Life and love," he added.

"Why are they the most important?" I asked, curious to hear his reply.

"Well, life is very important because without it, you can't do anything. And love is definitely important too. No love, no heart—no heart, no life—no life, no God!" he said wisely as I drove on.

"Interesting. How do you know this?" I asked.

"I just guess. Sometimes I guess and I'm right," he said while staring out the window.

I glanced at him briefly with a smile and then informed him, "I don't think you're guessing. I think you know exactly what you're saying. What we know comes naturally, from deep within."

The conversation ended before 8 AM as we arrived at the charter school.

Although the conversation above was with a child who was just ending first grade, the net value of that talk is the same for adults.

As you read, feel and examine the energy radiating from your relationship. Think about what you want from that bond, how you want it to grow and develop, instead of making it what's expected, like a predictable plot. You need to make your relationship be about you and your partner, in a non-reclusive and non-controlling way. You already have what you need.

There's not one thing that's a necessity in life that's not already provided to you. It's either all locked up in your inner-self, waiting to be revealed, or already exposed, waiting to be captured. Even the help that you should seek when things get unbearable is something that you must first accept from within in order for it to be effective. All you need to do is remember that.

This is where *Before SEVEN-THIRTY* comes in. It will remind you, by telling you of the ways the Universe guides you, and by showing you how to use the courtship signs to lead you to a healthier, more satisfying, and balanced relationship.

Chapter 3

CURRENT TREND OF MARRIAGE: QUICKSAND

THIS IS NOTHING new to many, but the signs of the times need our attention pronto. They are pleading with us to slow down and take notice. These signs have captured my interest for years, but it's only now that they want to come alive and take form as words. It's incredible how things occur in such synchronicity, which makes one wonder if life is toying with us sometimes. Carl Jung's soul must be smiling somewhere.

Most plays, movies, conversations, or articles that catch my interest lately have reinforced this phenomenon. Guess what? When it's time, it's time! I can't visit a major news network's website these days without seeing stories about couples calling it quits, getting a divorce, or entertaining discussions about relationships.

The headlines scream: *How to maintain a healthy relationship! How to tell if your partner is cheating!*

In my opinion, there is no denying that the collapse of the marital relationship has been the "It" subject for many years, third maybe only to politics and world peace in terms of things that are falling apart.

One minute, a couple seems to have a rock-solid bond, seems to have it all, then the next minute, you see the big headline, Star A Files for Divorce from Star B. You know how this goes.

These are just the ones we hear about because we are such intrusive beings when it comes to celebrities. For every celebrity divorce you hear about, there are hundreds more people divorcing on that same day. That trend continues. It shouldn't come as such a surprise, because we could hear divorce calling from miles away; however, we still are caught off guard by these announcements.

Our reaction doesn't come from having a personal relationship with these people, but rather it is because it's starting to sound like a game. Unfortunately, it's a game no one enjoys, except maybe the media because misery sells papers! Feelings get hurt, children suffer, families are destroyed, and husbands and wives become like moving pieces in a chess game.

We quickly forget we were once lovers.

Angry ex-wives might suddenly think of ways to make their ex-husbands bleed financially. Take him to the cleaners! Husbands might be devastated and try to get revenge by spending less time with their children or by not supporting them at all.

Who suffers the most in this bewildering scene?

Children are caught in the barbed wire as they try to escape the arguments and pain they feel when Mommy and Daddy are acting like Joanna and Ted from *Kramer vs. Kramer*.

Meanwhile, no one wins in this tragedy, except maybe the lawyers!

As you can see, it's not a game at all. Real emotions and real people are involved. Lives change forever.

There's nothing fun about getting a divorce.

Why is it so hard for people to stay together? What is missing?

One early morning, after having gotten into a heartrending argument, I had an epiphany. And my pen took over from there. *Before SEVEN-THIRTY* was born! Suddenly, it hit me. It's not that love and marriage are dead. It's just that people are sometimes oblivious to the factors that could later doom their relationships.

Following the footsteps of the persistent first US female private investigator, Kate Warne, I was curious and wanted to dig further. After all, if you start to see a continuity of events, then there must be a pattern, or at least something waiting to be realized. So I looked at the reason given in many divorce filings—irreconcilable differences. What does that even mean?

The more I studied myself in my relationships and the more I listened to friends who are involved, married, or divorced the more, I saw that many of us plunge into matrimony without first checking the depth of the water in the pool. We assume that just because there's water there it must be deep enough for us to dive in headfirst.

Let's go back for a second. Before we can acknowledge and understand the signs, we must first look at our history.

Since the beginning of our existence, humans have loved companionship. It doesn't take a rocket scientist to tell us that we are gregarious or social beings, which would explain why romantic relationship is such a hot topic. We cannot separate ourselves from it. We were created to have relationships, which is the basis for why we are forever seeking partnership. It will continue to be a part of us because it's built into our DNA: survival of the species. This is one underlying reason why people have taken such a hypnotized liking to the global social network mania. We want to be in touch with others, even if it's just a friend, a relative, a pet, or a stranger.

A perfect example of this was portrayed in *The Twilight Zone*—episode 1, season 1, *Where Is Everybody?* starring Earl Holliman, James Gregory, and Paul Langton (Serling & Stevens 1959). In this episode, an Air Force sergeant found himself wandering around town without anyone else in sight. He wasn't sure of his identity and desperately tried to find anyone to help him. Soon enough, he started to lose his mind as he yearned for companionship or anyone to talk to. The audience found out at the end that this was a simulation, with the sergeant in a controlled room with electrodes on his head and body, charting his reactions. He was in there for nearly three weeks, at which point he became delusional.

Having people to talk to, for no other reason than to have a conversation, is what makes us special and unique from other living things. Animals do not seek a "sounding board" or someone to "vent" to when they have had a bad experience.

However, the further we move away from nature (our mother equivalent), and hence, ourselves, the greater the separation will be from one another. It's a reminder that we don't speak the same natural universal language anymore. This disconnect is causing us to lose touch with ourselves, thus creating a domino effect on every interaction, including the relationships that we build.

It's a colossal understatement to say that we're at a pivotal point in the human race when it's so darn hard to maintain and stay together as a couple. People are becoming more apprehensive of marriage, and many are even waiting until their mid- to late-thirties before they get hitched. You may have heard of how some baby boomers are leaving their relationship of 30 or 40 plus years to enjoy some of what they've missed. These men and women want to do more for themselves since losing their identities in the name of matrimony.

The Evolution of Marriage

The quality of life has changed over the years. Marriage did not take long to reflect the evolution in social changes. But with that came the hard task of figuring out how we can continue to improve our quality of life and still have a happy home life.

Although the divorce rate is declining, it hasn't slowed down enough. The 42% to 50% divorce rate might be debatable, but there is no denying that the divorce rate is high for first marriages. Why is it still the case, despite the support groups, books, and marriage-counseling services available? What is causing this frequent dissolution of marriage?

Well, one reason could be that the dynamics, and what we want in a relationship, have changed over the years. What we are seeking from marriage has evolved, and so we must follow suit. Presently, many of us are looking for a lover to be our all, to be our twin flame, or to sweep us off our feet whereas in the distant past, marriage wasn't primarily about being in love, but rather its case was made for procreation or other external reasons. Both men and women are biologically attracted to those whom they see as fit for procreation. However, women want more than just having a husband, rearing children, and cleaning a house.

Let's take that even further, and I warn you that if you look up the etymology of marriage, you will see right away how our understanding of marriage has evolved through the centuries and why we must work three times as hard to prepare ourselves for this type of union.

According to *Merriam Webster Dictionary* online, first used in the 14th century, the word marriage's origin is from Middle English *mariage*, which is from Anglo-French, from whence *marier* to marry ("Marriage").

On *The AMERICAN HERITAGE Dictionary of the English Language,* marriage is described as follows:

Noun, 1a:

> A legal union between two persons that confers certain privileges and entails certain obligations of each person to the other, formerly restricted in the United States to a union between a woman and a man ("Marriage" 1076).

Wikipedia defines it this way:

> Marriage (or wedlock) is a social union or legal contract between people that creates kinship. It's an institution in which interpersonal relationships, usually intimate and sexual, are acknowledged in a variety of ways, depending on the culture or subculture in which it's found (2012).

So, marriage is legally viewed as a contract, even though we don't think of it that way because of love. But wait; can't contracts be broken if the right condition exists?

To break it down even further, it continues with Stephanie Coontz, author of *Marriage, a History: From Obedience to Intimacy, or How Love Conquered Marriage.* She explains it like this:

> "For most of our history, marriage was not a relationship based on mutual love between a breadwinning husband and an at-home wife, but an institution devoted to acquiring wealth, power, and

property. Picking a mate on the basis of something as irrational as love would have been considered absurd. Only in the nineteenth century did marriage move to the center of people's emotional lives, when the wife became the 'angel of the home' and the husband the 'provider.' Yet these Victorian ideals contain the seeds of today's marriage crisis. As people began to expect romance and intimacy in their marriages, their unions became more fragile" (2005 125-129).

Isn't it interesting how the ideal of marriage has changed so much over the years?

When you read about the history of marriage, it reinforces its base as an arrangement, whether it's verbally expressed or silently understood as such. People took their contractual obligations very seriously, or else there wouldn't be much to talk about today—the high divorce rate would be so passé. Men married to have children, or for paternity of their children, and women married to have a man care for them.

Before the feminist movement, women mostly stayed at home as housewives. They took care of the house, the children, and made sure that dinner was ready by the time their hardworking husbands got home. They weren't primary decision makers; it was widely believed then that the man was the head of the household. Yes, people had feelings for one another; however, the stage was set for many married people to fall into these accepted patterns. Generation Y, all 83 million plus, might frown, thinking this is all so plain crazy!

Another interesting link is that we use matrimony interchangeably with marriage. Again, *Wikipedia* and *The AMERICAN HERITAGE Dictionary of the English Language* both describe the etymology of "matrimony" as an English word that comes from the French word *matremoine,* which is derived from the Latin *mātrimōnium,* which combines *mater* meaning "mother" and the suffix *–monium,* signifying "action, state, or condition" ("Matrimony" 1084). But despite the original meaning of marriage, it means something much more to our generation than simply having a contract to procreate.

That could be one of the reasons why religion teaches that people should wait until after marriage to consummate their union. No marriage = no contract to procreate. No contract means no closing, which could be chaotic to peace, personal responsibility, and order. But what about the people who don't want children?

Having children may not be the number one reason as to why people get married, although it's part of the equation. Again, I think that since we broke away from the non-emotional connection of marriage, we are having a harder time satisfying the modern heart. A heart, which beats to its own rhythm and tells us that we need to be loved, be satisfied, and be happy when we are in a relationship. It's a beautiful thing only when it's understood.

So what can we do?

Well, we may not be able to explain why the heart makes us feel the way we do, but at least we can follow the signs, which speak a universal language.

Maybe only a few people really "fell in love" or there was a different meaning of this phenomenon in the past. You could have married because you wanted more wealth or prestige, because your prosperous or destitute parents forced it, you wanted to have a lineage or bloodline with a certain family, etc. But since we're expecting so much more from our relationship, it's causing the lasting effect to lessen, which creates more tension.

Furthermore, let's not forget that the responsibility scale has also shifted between men and women in the household. Women have had to assume more masculinity, which has the whole balance scale in a state of confusion. Should it tip left or right? Spring up or down?

Married life has certainly changed since the 1960s.

Our heart is the focal point now, and there's no turning back. Guys, go tell a female that you just want to marry her to procreate and see if you aren't left to drink your cold beer alone at the bar. Don't say I didn't warn you.

Although women are juggling the triple weight of being career focused, a mother, and a wife, men likely still marry for similar reasons since creation. Psychologically, they want to have that super wife with those physical attributes to bear children and to take care of the family. Even today in the 21st century, it is still considered a woman's responsibility to maintain a clean and hospitable house.

However, women have proven that they are just as capable of making great gains outside the home, although at a higher price. For instance, many women feel guilty or are criticized if they choose career over family or vice versa. The price? Women still have to be moms when they get home and continue to wear many of those old hats. Truthfully, we've just created more work for ourselves along the way. I am sure this was not what our feminist sisters intended all those years ago when they marched for their rights.

To our ancestors, happiness was seen in a different light then today too. The differences are plenty. We are a generation of over-consumption while our forbearers breathed a life of simplicity. We've expanded the meaning of happiness to much more than having a person who could provide for and protect the family.

For many of us today, our expectations of the relationship must be met for us to be satisfied. Furthermore, there's no sense of community like in the old saying that suggests it takes a village to raise a child. Since we are a people of independence, we're all about that in every way. We've broken the cord that made a place a "society" and, ironically, we are very disconnected from our neighbors despite the recent global social network takeover. We're more stressed out because we feel like we're doing it, raising our children and surviving, all by ourselves.

How Ill-Prepared Parents Add to the Dilemma

Where does a child learn to behave? Who is responsible for raising a child? Why is there such a surge in juvenile delinquency in certain areas? Where does a child learn to be a responsible adult?

Despite the adverse effect of some of the social changes on children, the start of the problem that young couples face today mostly began at home.

Yes, parents have a lot to do with some of the relationship issues that cause this chaotic trend that we face. A trend that's like having a blood clot, which seems to want to keep people from living a healthy and joyous companionship.

Have you heard the Eyewitness News catchphrase *It's ten o'clock. Do you know where your children are?* The family structure has changed so dramatically over the last thirty years. Do you know where your child is hanging out? Do you know whom your child is parading around the block with?

The issue is even more poignant if only one parent is around. There are many tired and overworked single parents raising children with very little support. The children are feeling left out because Mom can't be at two places at once. These children learn to take care of themselves very early too. It's not about a single mother not being able to raise a well-balanced child, but the issue comes when she has no help and is too exhausted to give her best at all times.

To exacerbate the situation even further, more absentee dads are not taking care of their responsibilities. And none of this is to imply there are no single dads out there struggling too, or reliable men that are there for their children. Of course, there are. But statistically speaking, our society sees more of the former.

I don't like to play the blame game, but in this case, I must state that some parents have dropped the ball too many times. These parents are trying to be on the runway while their children are just hanging out. They're not doing a great job being their children's role models and teachers.

I remember reading a book that stated that parents don't have to be role models to their children; their purpose is only to give them life. I would strongly disagree. Even though parents shouldn't be too intrusive, it is still their responsibility to help teach their offspring the ways of life and then let them ride by themselves.

It's disheartening to keep hearing of young people getting involved in gangs, bullying, and, lately, an explosion of gun violence in unexpected demographics.

It is understood that parents want better for their children. They work harder to provide more for their children, which in turn increases the chances of their children latching on to strangers for that unaccounted time and affection. Many parents don't have a work and life balance, which is preventing them from keeping up with their children's activities. When you add that up, you get a vicious cycle. Children are growing up too fast and are unprepared for the challenges they face. They are missing the good values and lessons that they must learn from childhood to adolescence to be responsible adults.

Parents must remember to teach their children about the trials of life and the complexity of an adult life, which includes a marital relationship. Of course, my mandatory expectation of all parents: have an open dialogue with your son or daughter.

It is important that parents minimize the effect of external influencers, such as troubled friends and the media, from raising their children. As a former single mother, I can attest that it is not so simple to keep our children on a constructive and rewarding road. I know of some parents who work hard and do their best to help their children learn to be responsible adults, yet these young adults choose their own dangerous paths. But we must continue to instill good qualities in our children, especially while they are young, which will help them later once they have a family of their own.

Some parents want to point the index finger to everyone and everything else—society, rappers, television, or video games—everything except themselves. So, parents, please put more effort into raising your children and less on the frivolities of life. Your influence in your progenies' life is more powerful than you could ever imagine. Both sons and daughters absorb the effect of how you act and what you do. More on this later.

Another major parenting issue is favoritism. I've witnessed some parents who ignore one child while they put most of their efforts into the other. Maybe one child is a quick learner while the other requires more attention. One child feels neglected and alone, while the other one prospers socially and academically. Something such as this might seem so trivial, but it plays a big part in how children view themselves as they get older as well as in how they respond to others.

Parenting has its challenges. There is no parenting rule book. Our instructions come from what we learned from our own parents and from others. Nevertheless, parents should be more conscious of the way they act, and how they treat and respond to their children.

The Universe:
Guidepost of Early Warning Signs

Yes, it's true that we are, for the most part, a product of our environment, whether it's where we grew up or who raised us. For those of you who are shaking your heads in disagreement, do you have a geographical accent? Or how about a sense of style, belief system, or a favorite cuisine associated with where you live, who raised you, or where you grew up? Maybe you've been told that you have a Northern accent, or that you must be from the South.

Regardless, we can choose to continue with what we lived as a child or upgrade it to something better as adults once we are exposed to more options and a healthier way of living.

We must look at all angles to see what is happening with marital relationships in our age and how we can help this generation, and the next, make more informed decisions. It's not too late!

But before we can do that, we must ask the right questions:

- Why do so many couples get the seven-year or rather the three-year itch more frequently than others?
- What causes the change of heart, since the majority of what we experience in a relationship is dictated by the heart?
- What is not present in a broken relationship that exists in a happy one?
- What is it that we're seeking that's so beyond our reach?
- Is it even possible to continue to navigate in that ocean of love, happiness, and fulfillment with our chosen partner, even through the extremely difficult times?

It's sad to say that, sometimes, the ones who are making it are not exactly swimming in a sea of bliss. Sometimes they do not want to disappoint people, or they are trying to prove that the marriage will last, albeit they are miserable and bitter.

A dear friend who has been married a few times wasn't delusional when he exclaimed during his interview, "A lasting marriage is not necessarily a happy marriage!"

Maybe we need to shift the way we look at our relationships and ask ourselves not how others define it, but rather, what it means to us. When we find another soul who sees it in a similar scope, then perhaps we will have something that will last.

As I mentioned earlier, another reason for this divorce epidemic, which many divorcées fall into, is the *I-ignored-or-missed-the-signs* category. Few people are talking about this major factor. Somehow, while they were dating and getting to know one another, they forgot to be attentive to their own needs and to their partner. They created an illusion where if things were not all right while dating then they would get better after marriage, or they think that they can handle the issues.

You can't possibly be for real! Remember the phrase *until death do us part*? While dating, if you missed some of the conspicuous signs that could later destroy your union, you might as well change that phrase to until irreconcilable differences do us part, or better yet, until unhappiness or dissatisfaction do us part.

If you decide to go the marriage route, then you need to understand its meaning. Take it from me, who's been there. Marriage, although considered a daunting institution to some, could be a gratifying beauty that marches to the drumbeat of each one of us who partakes in its daily dances. Whose beats are you marching to?

While some might look at an intimate relationship as if it's our worst enemy because it makes us feel so fragile and vulnerable, what they miss is the fact that it could be heavenly if we would follow what nature already provides to us. All we need to do is be more attentive and decode the signs.

The signposts pointing to either a healthy, great relationship or a miserable, downright unproductive one are forever showing face.

Dating does not automatically mean you will be lifelong partners.

I know sometimes we fall hard and forget to catch ourselves. Nevertheless, it's critical that when it comes to relationships, we brace ourselves before we hit the ground or else push with all our might to stand up if we do hit a snag. The clues to the eventual future state of our relationship sometimes scream at us, sometimes in our heads, and other times from our friends or relatives, and sometimes even from the partner that is doing the damage.

I even had a stranger show me the signs once after noticing that the guy I was with at the club just went incognito while other guys admired from a distance. It was painful as the other guy, who was having what seemed like the time of his life with his lady, whispered in my ear that I needed to ditch my dude because that was just inconceivable behavior. He too noticed what was going on. But Happy Feet, as I would like to call the guy who couldn't stop dancing, did not know that I was watching my then-boyfriend of nearly three years to see if we still had that spark since our relationship had reached an impasse. I was observing what was happening with no preconceived notion of what would come next. Well, let's just say the night ended on a very sour note.

Ultimately, we need to understand that there are signs to help us discern the messages hidden in the chaos. And you can't run from them because they are everywhere. These signs are actualizing The Principle of Cause & Effect. The people who see them are the ones that believe that nothing in life materializes by accident, that there are no happenstances. You have an option: from chaos comes either new creation (improved relationship) or total destruction (divorce).

Whether we choose to pay attention or not, every day is a journey to learning new things about our partner and ourselves. The syllabus is rarely ever blank but always tentative. If we would stop for a minute and analyze our lives and our relationship, to look for the signs when we are dating, then we would be able to work through some of these irreconcilable differences later. Most of these nuances would not be so "Oh My Gosh" and so new! They were present when you started dating, and they will continue to be until you notice them.

These differences are nothing more than just signs that you either ignored or put aside while dating. Unfortunately, many people acknowledge them after they have committed to their partner through matrimony. I'm not asking you to be a paranoid birdie, analyzing, questioning, and dissecting every last thing that you experience in your relationship. However, if you have been in the dating scene for a while, then you should get my point. You already know these signs, and I'm nowhere near describing them yet!

Don't let the divorce rate deter you from getting married if that's what you want. But you must take the first step, that leap of faith, right now by reviewing your relationship, since love is akin to risking and throwing caution to the wind.

You need to OLA: *Observe. Listen. Acknowledge.*

It sounds easy, but guess what? That's because it could be. The reason why a relationship is hard is that we make it hard. Like anything else in life, your relationship is what you and your partner make it, loving and satisfying or damaging and chaotic.

I naively chose the latter route in my previous life, but now I bid high for the former. I think anyone in their right mind would. It does not mean that you will have a perfect relationship, as we all have baggage that we could dispose of daily. These burdens create blockages, preventing us from allowing newness to come in and stalling staleness from leaving our being. We know what is crushing our progression to a happy relationship.

Any time you remove the heavy soot that you have allowed to accumulate in your life, even the hard stuff will start to appear manageable.

Picture this...

You look forward to the moment when you will see your partner. You had a long, stressful day and all you want to do is sit down and tell your partner about it. When you're together, it's like all that matters is just the two of you.

You can be yourself when you're around each other.

When things are not going well, you have each other as your picker-upper. When you get upset at one another, you know it will not last long because you're both aware that those little arguments are part of any relationship, but how or when you resolve them is what's important.

This person helps bring out the best in you when you're in doubt.

Yes, the best in you was there, but you might have been sidetracked for whatever reason. Maybe you took the road most traveled amongst your friends back in your wayward young days, and it is currently catching up with you. You did not think much about the future or about how your deeds could become a thorn to you later in life. You were a breathing robot, not really living.

But since meeting each other, your creative juices are flowing more. Your sweetheart challenges you to stop accepting less and take ownership over your life and of what's happening in it.

The energy is mostly positive when you're together. Yes, positive energy is that good feeling that you get in your gut, your heart feels light, and all worries are addressed or put aside for now. Listen to it!

How wonderful life would be if all relationships could be like this! No, this is not a fantasy. There are some couples who live that life.

Can you see yourself in that vantage? If so, you're fortunate to have met a partner to share such a wonderful life with you. However, many of us know that there are plenty of folks (both single and married) out there who are suffering and need a little nudge—I needed several—a reminder to address some of the issues that are killing their relationships.

It's just a friendly reminder. Hibernation or snooze time is up. Hey, don't blame me! That snooze button is tired of being hit time and again, only for you to reset it the next day so the battle can start all over again. Right now, I need you to do like Bill Murray in *Groundhog Day* and break that damn clock!

Go ahead, imagine yourself picking up that ringing clock and watch it follow the law of gravity as you exhale and smile while it breaks into pieces. Look at all the scattered morsels, each of which represents your letting go of an internal malaise, torment, despair, and dysfunction. Now, it's time to get things in order again. Ready, set…I know we're on the same page here.

Although a utopian world is eons in the past or future, at least we can choose to create our own personal heaven at home, right here on Earth. Now is the time, and the ring is loud and clear. However, that little piece of utopia will manifest when we admit that there's a problem.

My Eldest Son: I Will Never Marry

To me, the year 2012 was a period of letting go. One of the effects of the last major recession was that some people had to live from what I call PTP (paycheck to paycheck) while others became part of that more than 6 million unemployed trail. To complicate things further, there have been multiple divorces because of the strain caused by the drastic changes required when a financial crisis hits.

We all know that the problems were there before the recession, but you know how it goes. If you were on the edge of the Golden Gate Bridge and in great despair, it would only take the slightest nudge to push you over it. Likewise, I've also heard of many couples who had separated emotionally but could not afford to move out because of that economic meltdown, so they settled in the basement. I remember telling my ex that we should do something similar during our separation, years before the recent financial crisis, for our son's sake. But only a few special individuals can do that. We weren't of that special kind.

Fast-forward six years when my eldest son and I were having dinner one day and he expressed, rather unexpectedly, that he was scared to go to college. He was afraid that he would not be able to do his homework. So, I told him that was the reason why I make him focus on his schoolwork. Now is the time to build that strong educational foundation. What he learns from now until high school will set him on the right path of being ready for college or business school. He found that to be fascinating. Then I told him that one day he will do the same with his children.

That's when he turned to me and said, "I will never have a wife!"

Knowing my son, I knew there was more to this statement, so I probed. "Why not?" I asked.

He looked at me with those innocent chestnut eyes and said, "Because we might break up just like you and Daddy. Why did you and Daddy break up anyway? Could you not work things out? Were you fighting all the time?"

My son surprises me with what comes out of his mouth sometimes. Ladies and gentlemen, my son was only seven years old during this touching exchange. He was my little inquisitive *Curious George*.

"Did you and Daddy break up because I wanted more macaroni and cheese? Did you want me to drink milk, but he wanted me to have juice?"

I couldn't help but smile.

Despite having an old-man soul, my son was still an innocent child. Do you notice that he's talking about differences? I reassured him that just because things did not work out between his dad and me does not mean that he won't have a lasting relationship when he's older.

I expressed, as best as I could explain to a child, that I would teach him how to look out for some of the stumbles from my life and hope that he won't follow suit. Don't worry, he will get a copy of this book when the time is right.

Lucky for my son, I don't dismiss him when he has questions and is confused by what is going on around him. While I was growing up, my parents could have done a better job of showing how a healthy relationship between husband and wife should be. I guess they did the best they could with what they learned from their own parents. But my folks were very conservative and quite the non-expressive type.

They believed that if you're fed, have shelter, and go to school then that should sum up your life as a child. Their love was in their deeds, not verbal, or at least that's how my father used to put it. What else could you possibly want from your parents?

I, on the other hand, want to give my sons something extra: A life and relationship guidebook. There are many ways to get to one place. As my firstborn gets older, it will be his choice to decide which way he wants to go. As a parent, I have a duty to teach him what I have learned, both the good and the ugly, about relationships, so that he's not thrown out there without being ready to deal with some of the unexpected turns. Of course, I'm sure he will make his own mistakes since that's one way to learn. There's no guarantee as to how things will be once the 83 million-plus Millennials grow into adulthood.

I can tell that my former single-parent status greatly affected my son. Sometimes he used to break down, cry, and somehow manage to say that he wished that I were still married to his dad. Those moments were tough because the tears were so sincere. What I'm getting at is that most couples don't want to be divorced, especially when there's a child in the mix, unless you're a swindler. What, you think people spend all that money, time, and energy to have a wedding only to end it? Think again!

The real world is not like "Folly-wood" where some actors marry as if they are trying to catch up with all the stars in the galaxy. Outside the movie world, we marry because we fall for a person and think that we will be lifelong partners. I'm only talking about those who marry because of genuine reasons, rather than external allures, whether it's outer appearance, money, or some kind of gain.

We share a common link, no matter our outer differences, whether social, cultural, economic, religious, or spiritual. We want to be happy with the one we choose to be our husband or wife. Ultimately, we can break the current cycle if it's detrimental to a healthy bond and threatens the positive state of our companionship.

Your relationship doesn't have to end up as a statistic. I wish that my son didn't have to ask me questions about why my relationship with his dad didn't work out. I would have loved to have a unit where my son lived with both parents; however, I had to deal with my created reality.

After my divorce, I made a vow not to visit the same road that I took when I was an 18- to 21-year-old, who was a little lost and searching for something greater, somehow getting more confused along the way, unable to find my way back to true self.

It wasn't that I did not love my partner then. More pointedly, it was because I got married for the wrong reasons and had a lot to experience before I knew what life was about and who I was. Yes, the journey is endless, but I have since allowed myself to be more open to learning and exploring all that I could absorb about myself and my relationship.

So, we are on this journey together. The gifted author and actor, Hill Harper, penned that he writes to educate and to learn while in the process, and that's how I feel. There's no expert with all the answers when it comes to married life; it's so evolving and varies too much. You should take what applies to you and work from there. Regardless of what you have heard—and I must remind myself of this as well—there's hope.

Everything Has a Condition—We Experience It Daily

One Saturday afternoon, I observed this from inside a laundry facility: a young lady who looked like she was in her early- to mid-twenties was putting her clothes in the trunk of her car. Then, with obvious frustration, she lifted the empty cart with great haste and threw it up the divider. I was watching, not so much because she was too close to my car, but because there was a man in her car, just sitting there, chatting on his cell. A few more people watched with interest.

Meanwhile, her body language was expressing what she was feeling. It was obvious that she was not happy about something. When she got in the car, she immediately leaned her head against the window and started sky gazing. I cannot tell you how many times I have seen that look, when women just glower out the window or off into space with a blank glare as their lips pout in frustration. As if looking out at the passing sceneries will help ease their minds or take them away from their apparent miseries. Oh, that could have been me as well, except I'm usually the driver so I just stare ahead!

Naturally, I've observed more women than men waving their SOS flags because women are generally more demonstrative than men are. Meaning, you can look at an unhappy woman and you know.

Guys, that's how another man can swiftly pick up the unhappy signs from your partner and move in for the test. A man might front, but a woman's brows and eyes will tell the story. Now, if a man has been beaten up long enough (there are plenty of you out there), you may be able to tell as well. But generally, men like to keep their problems at home, out of the public eye, whereas women are more likely to create a scene. If we are unhappy, we won't sit there and smile, pretending that we are all right. Even if we try to fool the crowd, an Argus-eyed individual, ironically, it's usually another guy, will see the smoke of concealment and smell the funk beneath that phony smile.

At the end of the day, whether it's a man or a woman, we end up in such situations because we miss, or dismiss, the signs along the way and let things get out of hand. What we experience, even in those early months of knowing each other, is for something. There's a purpose to those important moments together. It's not only people that come into our lives with an agenda. The same rings true for our trials and hardships. Maybe we went through hell for a purpose that's greater than the now.

We may not know what it is at the present, but eventually, the pieces will fit. The effects could be fleeting, or they could change us forever. I remember the challenging time when I was mourning the loss of my beautiful canary bird and my beloved young cousin, as well as ending a draining relationship. Yet, it was worthwhile to go through that all at once. At the time, I couldn't see the light because I was depressed and in so much pain. But I know now why I had to go through that dark period. All three events symbolized a rebirth for me because I had to deal with the reality of losing what was so precious to me. Since those unhappy months, I've learned to appreciate life so much more and look at my experiences as my best teachers.

Similarly, the vibes from when you and your partner first met, and all the experiences while dating, are telling you something. Whether you pay attention and heed the signs, well, that's another story. And that's your story to set and resolve.

The signs do not care how you receive them. They will continue to show their prowess and will keep sending off their signals. They do not discriminate between the good and the bad. You will see both! This is why it is so crucial for you to have your eyes open because the signs are talking to you. Always! And they won't stop until you greet them.

The arguments are not happening for nothing. The breakups are not there just to make your life more painful. He's not leaving you at home to hang out with the guys without reason. Guys, your sweetie is not staying quiet or talking too much about her new friend, Stan or Scott, for nada. The clues are there right in front of you if you're observant about what your partner is communicating to you.

When we date, it is not just to get a free meal and watch a few movies, or to make another person go broke. I know there are gold diggers and players out there, but let's stick with the most. We date for a reason: with the intention of finding the person who will connect with us enough to become our long-term partner someday. Most of us don't court to waste time, although some people express right at the beginning that they're not looking for anything too serious. Most mature people date to eventually walk down the aisle and create a family. How far or close that ceremony is to becoming a reality is not what you need to focus on. You should instead look at the current state of your love affair.

Shouldn't the building start before you say, *I do?*

My God, what a thought!

You can't build a strong relationship on a weak foundation, a foundation that starts to take shape the moment you first meet, throughout the courtship period and onwards.

We all know the *Three Little Pigs* fable and how it ends. They may be childish, but there are great truths to all those crazy fables you read as a child. I promise if you read every single fable again, there's a lesson that you could use right now for the betterment of your relationship. Test it out and see!

These days people get married for a short time unlike in the past. Does the longevity really matter? Yes, it matters immensely, especially if there are children from that union. The children's view of what it means to experience life as a happily married couple is at stake if we keep gnarling at each other at this rate. Since divorce has such an adverse effect on children and home life, then for that reason it matters.

I think many couples would remain married if they knew how. It's not as much a fad, as many believe, to get married today and divorced tomorrow. Divorce is common, not because people don't want to stay married, but rather people just don't want to deal with the negativity and hard times. Not only has *until death do us part* changed, but also *for better or worse*. People today feel entitled to happiness without doing the work to achieve it. As I have stated, most of these issues started way before the exchange of vows. Paying attention to the molehills can keep them from becoming mountains.

Some would argue that there are more divorces now because the church used to dictate people's lives, and more people have turned their backs on God. I don't think that's the bulk of the puzzle. It's not exclusively non-religious people getting divorced. Even the ones who can't divorce because of religion or culture might be secretly asking how God could want them to continue to be with someone who mistreats them, abuses them, beats them, hates their presence, and crushes their happiness at every turn.

Your grandma might have been married for 40 or 60 years, but she also might have wanted to run by the second year, but she could not go anywhere. Many women were almost like chattels to their husbands. You can tisk all you want, but you took a history class. Don't tell me you were in the back row sleeping. What do you think the second wave of the feminist movement was about? But this, too, has exponentially affected the core of marriage today. Some women feel like they can be both the wife and the husband while some men are just idling and saying, "I thought women had it all figured out!"

Oh yes, there are some who follow the same path from centuries ago, as dictated by the church, even when they are unhappy, but that's by choice. We all have willpower and free will to make choices.

How many of you still use a typewriter? What about a buggy or an earth oven?

As time changes, people use the influences of that period to make decisions. It's not based on what one's great-great-grandmother did, but on what people of the current generation do. Previously, the choice could have been that no matter what happened in their relationships—the abuse, neglect, lies, and deceit—they would continue to stay true to that commitment. It wasn't to that partner, but more so to God and the sacredness of their vows, as they saw it. They were married to their spouses as well as to that commitment.

Yes, folks, they kept the faith even if they fell out of love or were abused while having faith.

We can't knock you for making your decision because, after all, it's your life. You have to live it. But the path you take is yours and yours alone.

Don't wait until you get to a Y intersection to decide if you should go left or right while there were signs showing that a fork was coming up, 1 mile, ¾ mile, and ½ mile away. You can choose, in this present time while you're dating, to create the life you want by working with your partner through some of the major hurdles, supporting each other to galactic heights, and understanding each other more. However, that's only possible when you become aware of the signs of doomsday.

I have observed how both men and women lose themselves in those crucial courting periods and just go gaga, literally. I know because I've been there a couple of times. It's as if they forget themselves, absentmindedly living a fantasy life; then the veil gets torn. Trust me, eventually, the veil will get a tear and will reveal the sunlight if something is amiss. So, when that happens, we need to be more attentive and readjust.

Doesn't it amaze you how good things are often tested? Well, that good thing might just seem to be that way because we were ignoring the issues. It doesn't mean that you should be a walking pessimist, but don't let being too optimistic inundate you with other disastrous things that are going on in your relationship.

For example, after my divorce, I thought I had created a peaceful environment at home. I warned any guy coming into my space to leave his BS outside the door. Initially, the relationship was cool, as he would try to be someone he wasn't just to keep me quiet or happy. So I would do my best to focus on this person's good qualities and I fought hard to get past his faults.

But it wasn't until much later that I realized that I had made a major mistake. My faux pas was in forgetting that sometimes the drama that people experience is also internal. So no matter how much I wanted the drama to stay away from my serene setting, the guy was carrying that drama inside him. So guess what? Eventually, the bubble burst and I had nothing but drama coming from all angles.

At first, I could not comprehend how that could happen. I had worked on creating this calm, drama-free world for myself by moving away from the chaos, but I found myself right where I started. Doesn't this remind you of the Law of Vibration (or Attraction)? The more you focus on something, positive or negative, the more you attract it to yourself. Anyway, that was my sign. Either I was going to pass or fail this test; those were my only two choices.

Interestingly, without that challenge, I would not have discovered that some men only tell us what they think we want to hear. Fortunately for me, with help from my cosmic friends, I eventually see the signs for what they are, and that's when I realign myself. We all must do this, or else we will fall into the venomous trap of discontentment.

Before the "I'm-so-sorry-but-I-don't-think-this-is-working-out" shocker, there are so many warnings that should have led to this realization. Well, remember the axiom *love is blind*. Sorry, you can't use that here. You can choose to fool yourself because your adrenaline was kicking in on overdrive and you couldn't think straight, but regardless, the other person could not keep up a flawless false persona. Of course, this is only true if you dated long enough. You chose to see what you wanted to see. Yes, ladies and gentlemen, you chose not to pay attention to, or react to, this person's conflicting ways.

Maybe you thought this person would change. Or maybe you figured what's a little rudeness? Besides, you like a man or a woman who shows their tough side; it turns you on! Or worse yet, you forced yourself to believe that love conquers all, without fully comprehending what that means.

It's almost like the inebriated man who is standing in the middle of the street hoping that the blind woman who is driving straight toward him will see him standing there and will eventually stop. There's a miraculous possibility that this could happen, but do you really want to take that chance? I can't picture too many hands going up to volunteer to be a guinea pig here. Why not just observe, take action, and be responsible for how your relationship turns out?

Remember OLA: *Observe. Listen. Acknowledge.* The signs of whether the marriage might end in divorce or not are usually staring at you, in the daylight or nighttime, during the dating period. You just have to open your eyes to see them and be realistic about what you feel and sense.

Despite the occurrences that will be out of your control, the Universe will give you a freebie to reconcile many issues before the big hoopla. Follow your instincts! Hopscotch back for a second to analyze your relationship. Don't be fooled into thinking that after matrimony these bad behaviors will simply sort themselves out.

So, it's not love but your lack of acumen to see that's blind. To me, real love, which not too many of us experience, and should not be confused with lust or infatuation, is an open, free-feeling vibration that sees and addresses all (very important) and doesn't hurt (crucial). The only time it should feel like it hurts is when you've lost a loved one.

Don't confuse the rush of endorphins as an allowance to go crazy. Will love be blind when you start to detest that person? I doubt it. Listen, even if love could be blind at times, the Universe will, in a flicker of a second, pinch your heart to tell you to wake the hell up. That's when we say love hurts, or we say that without pain, we can't truly love. In hindsight, it's just our misjudgment, not love itself, which makes us lose sight of the truth and accept what we see. All in the name of dear amore.

A couple of times in my life I thought I fell into this love-is-blind saga. But no, that was just me taking the long road home and letting my vulnerabilities get the best of me. My weakness is that when I love, I mean it with all my being. To some men, that's an incredible strength instead of a debility, but as an experienced woman, sometimes I feel otherwise. To love someone who causes pain can make you feel weak. After all, just like you, I'm not immune to challenges in my own relationships. I learned many years ago not to waste "I love you" on a guy who, based on his actions and reactions, gives off the air that he doesn't care enough to respect me or the relationship. So you can choose to see or choose to let the feelings lead your life.

Whether we understand the signs or not, they are there! When we think we're in love, we can do some crazy things to prove what we feel. To me, if it's true love then it should not change within a few months. However, it could morph like a beautiful butterfly as you mature in that relationship. Sometimes we might think we understand what it means to love someone until we meet a mature god or goddess who changes that narrow, superficial, and super-conditional love we felt in the past.

Amazingly, during your moment of daze, you will get a hint. A dear friend, a relative, or the butterflies from your solar plexus will alert you to address an issue. Don't ignore any of them. Best you deal with the issues now rather than wait until after you're married to learn that you cannot live with someone who needs to check into insanity rehab.

By now, you surely are asking what are these signs that talk to me? How can I make sure I do to not miss the signs and prepare myself for what's to come after matrimony?

Well, the signs are neither new nor that shocking. Like I said before, you already know them in your heart. You've talked about them. Sometimes cursed at them. You've even fought with your conscience when you had nowhere else to turn. You just didn't call them "the signs."

Take a second and ask yourself what some of the things are that have happened in your relationship that pain your heart. If you had one minute, how would you describe what you love best about your relationship? What would you like to change? Are the things that you would like to change a deal breaker but you're just too scared to take action?

When we grow too comfortable with a situation, it's hard to adapt to change. Complacency has a lot to do with the reason why sometimes we get stuck and just give up instead of strengthening our relationship right there in those crucial courtship months or years. But we cannot ignore how those periods before marriage are a precursor to what we have to look forward to. I must also assert that whatever is happening now will only intensify later on. So you should already have a list of your own warning signs before you read on. See how they compare with the ones in this book.

Chapter 4

SIGNS FROM FIRST YEAR
BEFORE SEVEN-THIRTY

THESE SIGNS ARE not in any particular order of importance. Each one has its own relevance that makes the whole—the break-up or betterment of your marriage. However, everyone has their own worries in life that are more pertinent compared to others. So as you read the signs keep that in mind. What's more important to you in your relationship? What can you tolerate and what is a dead zone?

I don't want you to start packing and run just because you're experiencing some of these issues, unless we are talking about abuse. That's not the aim of my book. But rather, I want you to assess and address. Work on the issues. Don't automatically think that the next person won't have similar quirks.

Relationship downers are followers. They will stick around no matter where you go until they are resolved.

Before people start to say that you're 730, wild or crazy, you need to catch yourself. Whatever you do, be honest with yourself and keep an open mind as you read on. Like any other dichotomy, you cannot be the only one who is willing to look in the mirror. So share your insights, and this information, with your partner.

There are at least three sides to what we experience in this existence. What we see and understand. What we can't see or don't understand. And the Truth. However, we relate to things through the limited lens of polarity, such as good or bad, right or wrong. So, although *Before SEVEN-THIRTY* focuses mainly on the chaotic issues, you should be aware that the positive signs will also be present. Cherish and appreciate those moments. Nevertheless, you must be armed with internal peace, wisdom, and love to face the destructive ones.

I will discuss the following signs and then funnel into some of the ways couples could keep their marriage alive:

- Communication issues
- Behavioral issues
- Past life issues
- Financial issues
- Criminal history
- Commonalities
- Boundaries

Chapter 5

OPEN EXCHANGE: HELLO!

ALTHOUGH WE HAVE evolved in many ways, there are two traits that remain fundamental to our kind: speech and behavior. There is not a day that goes by when we don't use them. So of course, one cannot talk about the human experience and relationship to one another without acknowledging them, whether directly or indirectly.

I didn't want to spend much time on this first trait, but it became mandatory for me to do so. Why? Well, because we just haven't learned from our own mistakes or from our parents' troubles.

Let's start with how much respect we need to give to communication. The continued advancement of technology has revolutionized the way we communicate and socialize. There shouldn't be a lack of communication in our relationships, yet this comes up repeatedly.

You have at your disposal one of the most incredible and powerful products in the telecom industry: mobile phones. With it you could call, e-mail, or text your partner, wherever and whenever. We are easily reachable. But I should warn you not to let this gadget get in the way of a good ol' talk.

The number of unique mobile phone subscribers in the world surpassed the five billion mark in 2017. As of August 2018, it is currently at 5.1 billion and counting. There are 7.6 billion people in the world (GSMA Intelligence 2018).

Have you seen how attached we are, especially to our smartphones? We have the popular social networking sites such as Facebook, Twitter, and Instagram where people don't even call anymore but they TTMI (Type Too Much Information) to stay connected. The problem? If we stay hypnotized long enough to these sources, we may become very disconnected from others when we have to make eye contact and keep the other person engaged. You don't want to have glossophobia. It's a horrible pain in the ass for anyone who wants to go out on a date at some point.

A cellular phone is a convenient tool to help you connect to others temporarily, but not to help you be lost in cyberspace when there is a real live human in front of you.

More important, you need to understand that no matter what, you do have to talk to each other in order for your relationship to survive. Communication will forever come up when you discuss relationships because that's our unique way of expressing who we are, what we want, where we came from, and where we want to go. It doesn't matter whether you use sign language or speech. Talk to any successful couple and this will be on their top five of what's important to a happy partnership. You will find a section, or reference, to communication in every relationship book that you read.

Respect Each Other's Voice

Can you talk to your partner with no reservations?

What does that mean? Well, it's simple: you should be able to say whatever is on your mind without suppressing the way you express yourself. I'm not talking about you cussing up a storm or having a fit as if you're going to war; you still need to be respectful. For longevity, you want a person who is willing to sit with you and listen to what you have to say without dismissing you. Do not minimize the value of each other's expressions. If either of you has a habit of cutting each other off, this is the best time to work on that because you will miss a lot.

So, when you hold back or cut each other off, you're missing an opportunity to have a two-way conversation. This is why people *co*mmunicate. It's a two-way street, not a one-way with only you on it.

Does your partner chastise or minimize the value of your expressions? It's not healthy for any relationship when you're dealing with someone who makes you feel like your words are worthless or just plain stupid. You know why you want to speak out or have a conversation.

Although you should agree to disagree, there's no reason to make each other feel diminutive because you think only your opinion matters. But I have noticed this more so when there's a clashing of values. If this way of reacting continues, then you'll miss the important details.

If either of you is doing this while still in your magical dating honeymoon phase, please speak up. Don't wait until you lose your voice and are married with children before you pull your that's-enough card. By then, you have invested so much time and energy into building what you have; that's why it's ideal that you do it sooner rather than later.

Do you even talk at all when you're together?

Have you noticed the couple who seems to want to escape each other every chance they get? It's a sign that these two people have hit a roadblock, either old or new, and neither one knows what to say to each other anymore. Running away is not going to solve the problem; staying quiet only intensifies the constricted energy. But how did it get to that point?

If this is a frequent experience for you, make an effort to initiate a conversation. When two people are together, whether it's at the dinner table at home, in a restaurant, or wherever, you should acknowledge each other at some point, and that's usually by talking or touching.

Do Not Shut Out Your Partner

Now, I'm not saying that you can't have some quiet or alone time, but if the reason for that is so that you can avoid your partner, you're creating a gap that could be avoided. Even if it's about how the week is going or the small ant crawling outside the window, talk you must. It does not matter what you talk about. This is important because it's how a couple gets and stays connected to each other's lives. If you're not talking now while you're dating, then you're only preparing your life for frustrations later as things get more intertwined yet separate after you're married.

What you talk about does not matter, but at the same time, it is important. You should be able to talk about anything that's on your mind, and similarly, you must pay attention to what is being said.

Are you able to find a common ground or talk about something that interests both of you? Are there some things that you cannot talk about because your partner has no interest whatsoever in those things, yet they are of great importance to you? It could be anything: educational goals, religion, spirituality, life, hopes, dreams, desires, or the future. So what should you do if you're the uninterested partner? We all need to learn to bite our tongue sometimes and just listen. Even if you don't agree, just listen. Actually, it would be a miracle if you agreed all the time because both men and women are misunderstood and sometimes feel confused.

I'm baffled at times when a man would dare say to a woman that he doesn't want her to share all her world with him if she wants to open up to him. But a great relationship can't work on only halves. A union must exist between you two. It doesn't mean that you have to spill every last detail of your waking hours, but you must combine your efforts to become whole concerning the bigger issues.

By the way, for those of you who love to play an undercover cop, it doesn't mean that you need to bug your partner's electronics or follow their every move daily like a GPS satellite without cause. It's not attractive. If anything, it's disturbing and troubling to think that you are with an individual whom you can't trust to even go from one place to the next without losing your mind. More on trust later.

Guys, a woman who enjoys having a little dialogue with you is something to be thankful for. You've been warned: The moment that you start to censor what she can share with you, you're welcoming a third wheel. If you won't give her your time, then she'll find someone else who will listen. And trust, he won't be too far. Just be careful when you start to limit what she can share with you! At the end (yes, there will be an end if you keep this up), you will be a lone wolf!

Distractions Be Gone

Don't wait until your engagement to look for these signs. Here is an interesting story that I heard on the radio on my way to the office one morning: a man wined and dined his girlfriend throughout the relationship. Then after one year of dating, he proposed. But he missed something that was a deal breaker for him—she could not cook. Don't laugh! This man came from a big Italian family where Mama cooked the big Sunday dinners and Papa kicked back afterward and smoked a cigar. Only after spoiling his lady and having proposed did he learn that she couldn't even boil spaghetti, nor was she willing to learn. He was ready to walk. This is not what he had imagined when he thought of his future wife.

Were the signs there all along? Did he ever talk to her about his childhood, the Sunday dinners, and how he wanted a similar life? What did they talk about throughout the courtship? Why didn't they cook for each other, at least once, during the one year instead of dining out all the time? From what I've observed, married couples don't dine out daily. Since this man didn't have plans to hire a chef after the wedding, this should have been communicated before the proposal.

To some people, this might seem miniscule, but to this man, this was very serious. But he only had himself to reprimand because he missed the many opportunities to get to know his girlfriend on a personal level before he got on bended knee.

It doesn't take a psychologist to understand that the communication part of your relationship, however it's accomplished, is a *must*. There's no way around that. You cannot have a stronger bond with your partner if you don't communicate with each other and hear each other out.

It's easy to get distracted. It takes great effort to acknowledge that maybe you aren't doing your best when it comes to communicating with your partner. It's not enough to just go out to eat and go to the movies, and not know much about what's going on with one another. Whatever is the cause of the distraction, handle it now. Whether it's your work, your friends, your family, or your own issues, don't allow it to take hold.

Another indirect distraction could be your lack of desire to speak up. If one of you is a recluse and the other is not, then you two need to find a mutual and effective way to communicate. From my experience, the person who is so quiet and reticent is sometimes difficult to get to know and even harder to connect with.

How can you understand your partner if there is so much about this person that is under lock?

I'm not talking about a shy person but rather someone who is holding on to some type of pain that prevents them from opening up to anyone. Imagine dating a person who is so reserved that you can barely hear them speak, even when you are sitting right in front of them. Yet speaking and communicating is so important to a healthy relationship. Again, if you find yourself with a person who doesn't speak up, find a way to break that barrier.

Although we can't all have the same gift, for those of you who want to lead a chaotic life by holding on to too much, you're not only hurting yourself, but you're hurting your partner as well. If you're confused about whatever, tell your partner. If you need time, let it be known. If you've reached the end of the road, express that! If you're pissed off because your darling doesn't show you enough of anything that makes the relationship worthwhile, set that rendezvous to talk. Because if it is only you who is always doing the talking or addressing the issues, then what is your partner up to?

Chapter 6

BEHAVIOR SPEAKS VOLUMES

BEHAVIOR IS THE most misunderstood characteristic of a relationship, the one that causes the most confusion. Ooh, but my partner makes me feel so good sometimes! Okay, that's all good for now, but wait a minute. Take a deep breath. Rewind past the bedroom. Think about what goes on outside of the bedroom. The world is full of many men and women whose love gets lost in sex. Some of you are thinking this should not be talked about, but get real. Don't be a hypocrite! Yes, you, hiding under the covers or behind that book! You know who you are.

Although bad sex can ruin a good relationship, it is not the main reason the divorce rate is high. If the decision were solely based on good sex, many of us would think twice before leaving our partner, especially when we're sexually compatible. It's mind-boggling how this one act can keep us in place even when the relationship itself stinks. However, good sex cannot save a lost marriage either. Don't let your carnal urges be the only good thing between you and your partner because your relationship will have little essence to keep it together for years to come.

Sometimes we allow our sexual satisfaction to blind us from the real issues at hand. A married friend of mine once said that people must separate sex from everything else that's going on in their relationship. I know that's not easy, but you must do that. If you want a long-term companionship, you can't focus on just one aspect of your relationship.

I know...the gods must be crazy! By now, you've learned that you can't just be all about the external appeals, and you certainly can't take care of only your carnal needs and pleasures. I'm not saying that you should ignore the importance of the intimacy between you and your lover, but sex should not determine the relevance of your relationship.

So what else should you be mindful of while you are in this state of euphoria? Well, I don't mean to fizzle your joy, but how does this person treat you? You've been dating for months, or perhaps years, and you know what's going on and what is not working. If you argue all the time or you just can't go through a week without fighting, then you have homework to do. Don't be the man or woman who tolerates anyone who treats you like refuse. And don't walk around boasting how you love your Mr. Wrong, Miss Cuteface, Mr. or Miss BangingBod. Eventually, people will get tired of hearing how you adore the person who treats you like dirt.

Yes, even your BFFs will go deaf after hearing you complain for months or years without making an effort to do something about the issues. It's the same crap being said repeatedly. I remember watching *Sex and the City* on syndication one day when Carrie Bradshaw, the journalist, kept going on and on about how her partner had just decided to move to Paris without consulting her, and my goodness she talked about him for days. Eventually, her three BFFs lost interest and had to tell her enough already.

The human heart is very selective, and we can become very passive. We accept certain conditions, no matter how unhealthy and costly, because we choose to. Our heart does what it wants even when we would prefer otherwise because it acts as if it's in charge. That's one reason people might say you have changed, softened even, ever since you fell in love. But you must remember that you pay for the decisions that you allow your heart to make without the benefit of consulting with your mind. So the next time you make a decision solely based on your emotions, check your heart and show it who's in control.

Early Patterns and Observations

Observe what makes your lover tick as well as how you're treated both in private and in public. I say this because at times your partner might make you feel like you're a god or goddess when you're out, but in private, that person is a dragon.

You have to listen to how you feel when you're together.

"How do I listen?" you ask. Well, similar to music, you have to tune in; in this case rather than a radio station it is your relationship and what is happening in it that you must dial into. It's not a coincidence that music is used as the analogy here because there's a deep connection between it and love. Music can brighten your relationship and connect your hearts so that even when you're miles apart, the moment you hear a song, you instantly smile and think of that person. Music is the language of love! Let's get back to that later.

Can you be yourself or are you guilty of identity theft, assuming a persona that you don't even recognize just to appease your significant other? Don't be stuck like a damaged disc, just playing a repeated role. Eventually, the true you will unleash itself, and you will be sorry that you were imitating and not living your truth. There's no exception to this. You can be an actor, but only for so long. Even the best actors must retire someday.

So embrace who you are and do away with allowing just anything to happen to you so that you can be in a relationship. Remember that a relationship doesn't breathe and is not effective until we make it so. Meaning that your relationship will take whatever path you want it to take, healthy or unhealthy. Everything that happens during your partnership falls under either one of those two states.

I've heard stories about couples belittling one another. Are you in one of those relationships where your partner puts you down, makes you feel non-existent, and verbally abuses you? Clearly, that can't be a good sign. An occasional spat is common, but if this person is making a habit of putting you down, then maybe it's time to reconsider your relationship. You should expect respect and give the same.

For instance, imagine this sad life of a young couple where the husband felt like he was the king.

Side note, a king better recognize when he's also dealing with a queen. But I divagate.

So, this man wouldn't take his wife anywhere, and if they did go somewhere, he walked five steps ahead of her. Strangers and friends had his attention but not his committed wife. She sat at home, cried, and frequently asked the damaging question, "What is wrong with me?" He dismissed her as irrelevant while at home and ignored her when out at special events.

How does a relationship get to such decay?

The crazy thing is that when men hear this story, they often ask about the wife's appearance. Is she fat? Is she pretty? Like, really, what the hell! She's his chosen wife. Doesn't she deserve a little attention, love, and appreciation from her husband?

This is a marital problem, but that does not mean there aren't any men and women who are experiencing this while dating. If you do see this sign, handle it. Do not wait for it to get to the point where you're chewing away at your own self-worth later on—stand up for yourself now. How are you going to stand if you don't love, accept, and cherish yourself first? If you don't know how, then I suggest you go to the "I AM NOT" section (p. 139) before you proceed. You may not be able to control another person, but you do have the power to ensure that what you receive from your lover is nothing but the best. How? By stopping bad behaviors in their tracks. Don't let things escalate to the point where they are out of control. By then, the damage may be too severe and already engraved in your daily life.

Bad behavior can breed stress for the recipient, and that can make that person ill. So let's minimize our visits for medical checkups by reducing how much of such behavior we permit to invade our homes. There is no better time than when you're dating to observe how your partner treats you.

On the other hand, you should also pay attention to yourself and your behavior. If you feel like you're a time bomb ready to explode at any moment, then learn to manage your temper. Please don't lose your cool in public. Just don't, especially if it's about something inconsequential or petty! If you need to address something, wait until you get to your car. There's no need for others at the grocery store, the liquor store, or the restaurant to hear your personal business. We need to take a better hold of how we treat each other, starting now.

My long-lived advice: Don't take your loving partner for granted because you will regret that when you find you no longer have a loving partner to take for granted.

Physical Abuse: No More Tears

Anyone who knows me well will tell you that I have a soft spot for physical abuse victims. I remember when I was around 11 years old and I told my father that I didn't believe an adult should ever hit another adult. I was young but wholeheartedly believed in what I said. If you want to see me get emotional quick, show me a movie with such and I'll be in tears in seconds. So I don't watch movies that show a woman being abused.

Women are generally raised to be nurturers, which is natural and good; however, do not allow your Mother Teresa nature to cloud your judgment. It's one thing to be caring and sympathetic, but remember to be on the alert when your partner starts to exhibit an aggressive behavior.

That doesn't mean that abusive relationships are all the same. Some females are just as abusive, so if you're a man and you're allowing a woman to abuse you physically then you have the same responsibility to yourself to get help, even if it is hard to admit. No matter who is on the receiving end, we should not find this as acceptable.

You would be amazed at the number of young people who are involved with an abusive partner. According to the CDC 2017 Youth Risk Behavior Survey (YRBS) Results data, 9.1% of female high schoolers and 6.5% of male high schoolers reported being physically abused ("National Center for HIV/AIDS, Viral Hepatitis, STD, and TB Prevention" 2018). What a pity! Many youths are so ashamed that they keep it to themselves. They claim to love their partner so much plus they promised they wouldn't do it again.

I highly doubt that an abuser will be irascible or hot-tempered just once without intervention.

I always promise myself that I won't cry, but my tear ducts speak a different language. If you haven't seen *What's Love Got to*

Do with It, I suggest you check it out, especially if you're in an abusive relationship. As the title proclaims, love has nothing to do with being abused. To love someone is to want nothing but the best, to protect, to serve, and to cherish your bond by mostly allowing the positive rays of light to hit your union.

Physical abuse is, and has always been, about power and control. People who are being abused are giving away their power and have lost control over their lives. Do you know who you are? Do you know how powerful you are? Are you aware that you're responsible for taking care of yourself and making yourself happy?

Abusers love to run with it when they meet anyone who is weaker, vulnerable, or just too kind to give up hope on helping the one they love. And these are the ones who often end up in such relationships.

Those who are enervated or vulnerable are preyed upon because the best time to beat a victim is, you guessed it, when that person is already down. We all have weaknesses, but it should not be a ticket to Beatdown Ville. Your foibles are there to teach you lessons and make you stronger, not for others to feed on. So, you must recognize their existence, or else you could fall prey.

Your weakness could be anything from fear, to codependency, to an over-abundance of desire to help your abuser who manipulates you in order to stay and help get things right again.

The fear could stem from a previous relationship or from childhood. Maybe a subconscious, irrational part of you thinks you don't deserve better and wants to keep you from moving forward. You have now become one with negativity. You have sadly become accepting of this parasite and joy killer. After all, maybe that's all you have ever experienced from those who have said they loved you. So now you don't know how to welcome a better life.

Codependency is self-explanatory. Maybe you feel like you need to have approval or a go-pass from your partner about the simplest things. It's hard for you to stand on your own because you believe that you just can't do anything alone.

Are these the kind of thoughts going through your head? Seriously? Don't you think that you could be a lot better off, and happier, without all the pain? Remember that this is all a test. This is you challenging yourself to see if you have taken heed and have listened to that inner voice that is calling you to see the light.

If you think of the people who come into your life as teachers, regardless of the lessons, then you could quickly nudge yourself to stop accepting pain and sadness. Why do you think that many people who have suffered, or have experienced an ill or an ethereal phenomenon, most often turn into advocates? You have the power to change your life to your satisfaction. It begins with sitting down, clearing your mind, putting your problems on the table, and listening to the answers from the Universe. Do not forget your own happiness at the expense of someone else's dis-ease and lack of self-love.

Sometimes you might find yourself sacrificing your happiness just to help an abuser who knows that you will forgive them because you've been down that same road many times before. After all, you've been told to stand by your man/woman through thick and thin, and to forgive. But at what cost?

The abuser studies your weak points, whether it's a kind word, act, or make-up sex. They might even help you nurse your wounds after committing such an offense just to show you that they care so much and that they need you. They might even tell you that they can't be without you.

Yet again, how quickly they forget the next time they get angry, reminding you that you made them this angry and are the one to blame. Subsequently, you feel stuck, not able to remove yourself because of what you feel for this person.

The secret to personal freedom? Know your own weaknesses and don't feel ashamed. Shame will keep you from progressing. Write them down if you have to, and then take action, so that you can start smelling the roses or enjoying the sound of the birds chirping on a sunny, breezy day.

This is not an attack on the ones being abused. It's an alarm to let you know what time it is. Time to build yourself up! Rise up and revert your thoughts to sensing yourself in the present. Can you feel and hear yourself breathing? Now, start building!

Abusers are predators, and they know exactly how to continue with the cycle as long as you're allowing it. It's distressing that people who are dating or living together will allow this. Allow is the right word because a person cannot abuse you like a bad habit unless you allow it to continue. Did that person hold a gun to your head or drug you with a Mickey? Fear of worse if you leave is not a good reason either.

Allowing yourself to be a victim is not helping your cause and purpose on this beautiful Earth. Remember that you can be your own setback to having the type of life and marriage that you've always dreamed of. You do that by forgetting to realize your Self.

Those in such predicaments might say, with great annoyance, that I just don't understand because I'm not in their shoes. Well, that's true, but do you even understand? I would like you to explain then what's so healthy about such relationships. And yes, if a predator does it now, then trust and believe it will continue and may become worse while you're married, unless you put an end to it. You can be tolerant, but not gullible.

Let's see, you say, "He loves me but then turns around and abuses me. He loves me but then wants to see me hurting and in pain. He loves me but then wants to control my every move." How does that sound to you?

Watch out if you're already experiencing this type of behavior while you're dating. Once we start to date, we become lax, let our guard down, and accept things that would normally be a turnoff. Make moves now! Since you haven't tied the knot yet, then you had better run. Run to find a solution or race out the door and don't look back. Do whatever it takes to STOP it, not after you're married or land in a coma. *Now* is the time! Well, *then* was the time, but since it has already passed, we must settle for *now*.

I'm convinced that abusers are people who don't love themselves. They have forgotten how to love in a healthy way. They are afraid, insecure, and feel powerless from within, and attacking others brings them a false sense of empowerment and strength. Whenever there is a lack of anything, especially the essential love for Self, then it could become a facility to hurt another being.

Do not take this behavior lightly, as if it's nothing, unless that's how you want it to be. You need to be a fast learner. Don't keep walking on the Penrose's Stairs, or the never-ending staircase, unless that's your wish. Otherwise, make it your duty to want better for yourself. Now. Think about your future. Do you want a life void of your power and self-worth?

Mental and Emotional Torment

Mental and emotional abuse: many people don't acknowledge them as much, but they're insidious siblings of physical abuse. Notice that I didn't say cousins, but rather siblings of physical abuse. They are that intertwined and just as venomous. Your physical state is a result of your mental and emotional states, so if you're emotionally and mentally sick then you'll feel it physically. You already know this, but sometimes you forget this simple fact.

When I'm hurting or feel depressed, I get bad headaches and then start to lose my voice, as if I'm coming down with the flu. It's downhill from there. You can see it in my eyes, as noted on many occasions by others.

So how does one abuse the mental and the emotional?

I'm sure we can all think of a person who is a pro at this. You know the ones who call you derogatory names; aliases that turn your smile into a frown. The ones who tell you that you will never be anything great in life.

If this is the case with you, your partner might have their own emotional or mental issues that they are projecting onto you. This is why you must beware and not become the next victim. This is a habit that you don't want to befriend. It will not only become second nature to you, but it will also slowly deplete your self-esteem.

I've learned that anyone who is commenting about your looks and rarely has anything positive to say is putting out their self-image. No person would look at another and think something negative unless that negativity comes from within. But if you have inappropriate comments swirling your way on the regular and you take them personally, they will affect you. They will cloud the positive things that are happening around you. So, if you're experiencing this emotional, and eventually mental, drain then express how you feel about it.

How do you see yourself? Are you beautiful or handsome? Special, with a purpose? Unique? People can often notice your thoughts and feelings by how you view yourself. Rarely will you see a secure guy disrespecting a female who carries herself with equal respect and pride.

Similarly, a single woman or maybe a married one will notice a guy who walks into the room holding his head high. His confidence is demonstrated through his walk and the way he makes eye contact. Think of the Denzel Swagger! Now, I don't want a bunch of Denzel clones faking the swag. You have your own—find it.

It's the perfect time to stop your partner from attaching a bad habit to your relationship. A great partnership requires that you both work on your own mental and emotional state and help the other heal accordingly when necessary. This is not the time for recess, but rather, for excess of support and bonding.

Hello, Darling, Remember Me?

Wait a minute! So besides trying to shrink your self-esteem to null, now your partner wants to ignore you too? You know you can't have that. Really, did you forget that you have company?

I'm not a hopeless romantic, but I do want my presence felt when I'm with my partner. Don't you? No, I don't want him to just sit there and stare at me, but I do want him to acknowledge that I'm there.

Take time out from whatever you have going on to appreciate one another. Some would argue that a guy who ignores his girlfriend is trying to tell her something. Namely, that he just wants to kick it with her and nothing more. Those who read *Act like a Lady, Think like a Man: What Men Really Think About Love, Relationships, Intimacy, and Commitment* by Steve Harvey will know what I'm talking about.

You don't need to throw a fit because your partner is engaged with something else. However, if you are together and his attention seems to be anywhere but on you, every time, then you might have a problem. Especially if it occurs frequently outside of activities such as watching a movie or a game. It would be awkward if you were just sitting there staring into space while in the same room your partner is very much alert to other people, situations, or activities.

How beautiful it is when two lovers share a moment together, but if you can't stand each other's company while you are dating, then imagine how married life will be. You could find yourself with a husband or wife yet feel single.

Would you ignore your friends or houseguests? Then why would it be strange to think that you should keep your wife or husband company when you are together, and the moment is right for some tenderness and loving or simply a few words or simple touch?

Acknowledge that your lover is present. Do not get into the routine of ignoring each other.

I'm Bossy, Says the Parrot

Lovebirds, when you are around each other, keep it light and simple. To ignore your partner is one side of the coin, but on the other, some people want to argue about every damn thing. In those cases, you wish your partner would just ignore you. Neither one is a good friend. Many of you have heard of, or you know, someone like that. It's as if arguing is their high. Having a debate can be fun, but come on. Who wants to be around a combative person who is frequently shouting down their ideas or thoughts? Such moments are a waste of energy as you desperately try to get your partner to understand you.

I know of a few relationships where the wives act as if they live on planet TTDM (Talk Too Damn Much). My God, it's as if the men can't do anything right, and you can tell that sometimes they want to break free from that loud and overpowering woman. This usually happens when the guy is reserved, and the wife is boisterous, thinking she's the omniscient CEO. Since she has voted herself as the boss, she pulls the strings whenever she likes. When you see these men, they look pitifully drained and tired.

Ladies, you had better sing your "Bossy" song under your breath and loosen your grip because most men don't want to be with a bossy woman. Pretty soon, your partner will be singing "Bye Baby" in return.

At the end of the day, just do your part, not both, and wait for your partner to meet you with their dues. Stop the urge to argue about the little things. Who wants to live on a battlefield? Either way, you could end up solo if you keep any of that up.

Behavior, whether constructive or destructive, can tell you plenty about a person's psyche and view of self and the world. Don't downplay bad behavior while you're dating. Also, don't think that you can be Dr. Psyche where you can simply talk this person out of their ways. If it's a major behavioral issue, which could be any of the ones discussed in this section, then consider external help, especially if you need to repeat yourself multiple times about the same issue.

Chapter 7

LIFE REGRESSIONS

THIS IS A hard and complicated truth to swallow, yet, the health of our relationships could well depend on it. The parental relationships in our childhood are the prerequisite views of our adult lives. Some may disagree, but more would concur, that what happens in our tender years will help or hinder our intimate relationships. If a child constantly misbehaves or is just a delinquent, what's the first thing that comes to mind?

Think about it.

What was your childhood like? Was it easygoing, fun, childlike, and happy? Or was it more depressing, hard-knock, disastrous, and empty? If you're honest with yourself, you can see how your childhood is affecting you. Maybe you did think about it but still could not pinpoint why your relationships have been so empty, disastrous, hard-knock and depressing. Get it? You're simply reliving your childhood relationships without taking ownership of your adult life. Knowingly or unknowingly, you're battling with those issues daily. We often swear to ourselves that we will never be like Mommy and Daddy but turn out just like them. Why?

Well, because their actions left an imprint on us on a deeper level. Yes, life is about growth and maturity. A bad relationship between Mom and Dad doesn't always have a direct link to your adult life. But there can often be lingering residues clinging to your psyche, especially when your childhood experience was a calamity. This is not about rehashing other people's beliefs; it's just a simple fundamental truth of life. Nevertheless, as adults, we must be honest with ourselves and set our hearts free if we want to enjoy the best fruits of life.

Think of it this way: As newborns, our first bond and awareness is usually our mom as we become more cognizant of our environment. This begins the cycle that takes us to the different phases of our lives. As adolescents, we form either a healthy or unhealthy relationship with our parents. As adults, we continue to yearn for companionship, albeit this time on a different and intimate level. We will emulate in our adulthood what we saw at home as a child, whether consciously or subconsciously, good or bad.

There's a reason why you absorbed so much as a child. Those experiences were inescapable and indispensable to your personal path to adulthood. When much younger, my fourteen-year-old son's worries in life consisted of not having enough time to watch TV, not being able to stay up late, or losing his toys. He paid attention to my actions and words as he tried to understand this world. My son would question me until my explanation made sense. "Why, Mommy?" was a constant in my world.

An event doesn't need to be epic for it to have a lasting effect. It just needs to have importance to the child in some way. Go back to your childhood for a second. Remember how you adored your mom and dad. You would run to them the moment they opened the door after a long day at work. You cried when left with a babysitter. Mom and Dad were your world. When you hurt, you went to them. When you felt sad or upset about something, you made it known to them. They hugged you, reprimanded you, or taught you new things.

Your being was recording every moment. As an adult, you revisit these moments, except now, you view life with a more serious and mature set of eyes. If your parents were supportive and loving, then you will expect the same from a partner. However, if your parents or caregiver was very remiss, you might hold on to resentment.

Thus, if your childhood was not so exemplary, but rather full of disparagement and very little affection, then you must release that negativity in order to develop into a healthy adult. Sadly, sometimes if we were raised in such an environment and we later meet a person who treats us in a loving and respectful manner, we unconsciously sabotage it just to get that familiar negative reaction. This is called cognitive dissonance. What we really seek is the love and support that our partner is giving us, but it's unfamiliar, so we don't know what to do with it.

You need to decide to discontinue that negative cycle, because if you're still encased in those pains, not only will your spouse feel the effects, so will your children. The outcome could be positive if you realize that you should change your thought patterns and attitude about your past. However, the opposite could also exist if you try to cover it up.

For instance, some people overcompensate for their lack of a wonderful childhood by contributing to the nag-factor. They promise to do better than their parents but then end up doing just the opposite. And so the cycle continues. Haven't you noticed how people who are pro-corporal punishment use themselves as an example of how they turned out all right? So isn't it time to make amends with your life regressions?

Partner's Childhood

A person's primary attitude toward their relationship comes from home. Knowing this, it's only fitting that you do an aerial view of your darling's life by asking some questions. What is the relationship like with Mom and Dad? What were Mom and Dad like while your partner was growing up? Are they around? How involved are they in their son/daughter's life?

By the way, if the current relationship between parents and son/daughter is on bad terms, then you must find out what happened. Listen to what you are told.

In life, we sometimes get a second chance to fix things that went wrong due to what seemed like happenstance. But we can only repair and heal ourselves once we're aware that we are hurting, whether emotionally or mentally. For instance, if while growing up, a man had a healthy and happy relationship with his mom, then he will want the same from his girlfriend or wife. It's a truth we can't escape. I've felt and lived with the effects of the damage caused by this black hole in men and have seen what a lack of parental love does to women too.

On the other hand, if your partner doesn't care for their family, that is a huge red flag as well. The relationship between son and dad, daughter and mom, and vice versa, is somewhat indicative of what you have to look forward to as a couple. However, it could be different if you consciously choose to stop the cycle.

One day, while nursing myself, I watched the movie *I Never Sang for My Father*, based on the namesake play, starring Melvyn Douglas, Gene Hackman, and Dorothy Stickney. Gene Hackman's dad, Melvyn Douglas, was a bloviating, pompous, and domineering man that barely knew his son. On the other hand, Gene had a very loving relationship with his mom and his fiancée. However, he was troubled because there was this boyish behavior about him whenever he was around his dad. He was a "yes man" when it came to his demanding father. Gene's relationship with his fiancée was similar to the bond he had with his mother. He treated his fiancée with the same love and fondness that he had for his mom (Cates 1970).

Mom & Dad: Lifetime Influencers

When was the last time you heard a woman say she does or doesn't want a guy who's like her mother? It's her father she will compare her partner to. A woman might have a hard time if you start reminding her of the dad who didn't show her love, made her feel so insignificant, and told her she was deficient. Or if you show her too much love, she might freeze at first. It might take her a minute to grasp that it's all right to receive love and support from a man. That reaction is ingrained from childhood.

One of three things will happen. Either she will be attracted to the kind of men who remind her of the dad whose ways she was trying to forget, or she will only date guys who are nothing like Daddy. Or maybe she will fall for the guy who is a little bit like Dad but who also has other favorable attributes.

However, sometimes we think we have chosen a man who's nothing like our father, but he turns out to be similar in a different way. What I mean by that is maybe your father was an alcoholic, but the new man in your life doesn't drink. Give it time; you may find out he is a workaholic or perhaps a gambling addict instead. He might even be addicted to healthy living and working out, but if it serves the purpose of making him emotionally or physically unavailable to you, it is really the same result.

It's your responsibility as a partner to be aware of the signs that something is not right. The signals could be anything from temper tantrums, abandonment, lack of ambition, lack of caring, drugs, etc. Be ready to deal with them. For many of us, our childhood days were not so posh and majestic, but it doesn't mean that we can't fix what needs TLC now.

Understand that we all have the power to heal the destructive experiences of our youth. But we can only do that when we pay attention to who we are and where we came from. Most of us will live a life similar to our parents. We will do some of the same activities that we used to do with our parents, and we pass on the same to our children.

This is why life regression is so vital. You need to know whom you're dating. Find out what that person's life was like before reaching adulthood. Many people might think it's trivial but how did you get to be who you are today? Did you just wake up as an adult without traversing all the phases of life? We need to put our childhood in its proper compartment, but many of us fail to do this. Knowing will help you piece the puzzle together when you need to understand why your sweetheart reacts a certain way at times.

Some mothers may have been lacking in caring the way a mom should, perhaps because they were doing it all by themselves, or they were just too young. Maybe Dad wasn't around or didn't have a meaningful impact in his children's lives. So, since childhood, a son or daughter builds distrust, not understanding why Mom ignored their needs or Dad seemed to have forgotten their address.

These deep wounds expand until there's a big break, like addressing them. You can be 50 years old, but if you lived life as above, the pain is still with you. Symbolically, like a tree that will transform or die if you uproot its trunk because it requires root for survival and growth, we humans have the same connection to our roots, where we came from. The tree may reproduce, and the cycle could continue, but the damage is already done.

Our root, like the tree, is our parents.

The heart rarely forgets what pained it. If anything, it builds a protective shield so that it doesn't ever hurt that way again. You can be grown but cry like a child when your parents hug you, say that they love you for the first time, or apologize for the past growing pains—where you actually hear the words, *I'm sorry.*

If you are a single mother, like I was, you can do your best to help your children grow into upstanding citizens, but ideally, you still need help from Dad. This is why I don't believe that a mom should ever keep children from their dad, assuming that he is safe, and willing, to take part in his children's development. It's imperative that we don't let our young jewels suffer because of our issues with our ex. If there is no way to have Dad involved, look into mentorship programs for your children; organizations like Big Brothers/Sisters are there for these very reasons and can make a positive difference in your children's lives.

But also be wary of putting that fatherly responsibility onto the new guy in your life. It's not your boyfriend's job to be your children's dad if the biological dad wants to be in his children's lives.

If your destructive past is left unresolved, you may feel like your partner doesn't truly care, that your lover might desert you, or that you can't give your all to anyone. It's time to hit the brakes and take control of your life.

Look at yourself and heal any anger or resentment you might be carrying around from childhood. If you are angry at Mom because you feel that she did you wrong, then call her. If you have nothing but contempt for your dad, then talk to him. Maybe you will learn something about yourself, and your life may start to make sense.

Childhood Abuse Issues

Are there any childhood abuse issues to address? This is an emotional and personal subject to many. However, if these issues were not healed through therapy or any other modality, then get help. You're doing yourself and your partner a great disservice if you keep ignoring or running from those deep issues. Work on them now, before you marry. Find the appropriate time to talk to your partner about them and discuss how you have managed to deal with those childhood pains.

Unfortunately, the scars don't ever go away until you get the help you need and move toward living the life that you want. Not healing may cause you to lack confidence and become very disconnected. The same is true for guys who were abused as children. It's not just little girls whose trust gets stolen. We're hearing more than ever about little boys in the news. It's hard to know whom to trust. Sometimes, it's shocking to learn that the person you trusted the most with your child is the predator. These are hard times for parents and children.

Children are innocent victims, but as adults, they must take control, heal, and free themselves from past afflictions. Past issues are never truly in the past unless sorted through and left there. Be kind to yourself by not blaming yourself for what happened. Whether physical (severe to extreme—more than a light disciplinary pat on the behind) or sexual, abuse is abuse. It causes serious damage to a child's self-esteem. It messes up the innocent and happy stance that children should have about life. The effects will whirl into their future like a slow-moving yet deadly tornado.

But as adults, we can take the reins and do what we must do to mend our broken hearts and strive for a healthier relationship by getting help and living in the present, poised for the future. You have to think about how this will affect your relationship with your partner. It will no doubt have an impact if left unresolved. So, healing now is doing so for the peace sake of your future.

If this is resonating with you, then seek counseling. Your partner might not know how to deal with something of this gravity, so see about getting yourself right first so that you can be prepared for your lover's reaction. It's the best present you could give to yourself.

The Lot of Our Day

Speaking of the past, are you comparing each other to your exes? The moment that a man starts to negatively compare me to an ex, I would leave him right where he was standing. No two people are ever exactly alike. Get it right! I'm not Barbie, Zoë, Shaniqua, Tameka, or Kylie! Although interconnected with all, there's only one ME!

Yes, what you experienced with your ex may have an impact on your current relationship. But to be in comparison limbo is to imply that you haven't progressed or moved on emotionally. If you keep going through the same struggles in every relationship, then it's not your significant other, it's you! It doesn't matter how wonderful the new partner, the same issues will continue to arise. So you need to get rid of that pattern. Think about it hard, and you will see why that has been happening to you.

We are all on a journey, albeit different for each individual. Each one of us has to cross that bridge called *Learning*. The route to the bridge may not be the same, but we must cross it if we are to mature into a grown man or woman. Some people never make it across, while others linger longer but still find their way. What's mandatory is that the person eventually learns that life is a journey with unexpected courses and sudden darts on the road.

So if people are naturally different, then what are you comparing?

To think that our partner is an avatar is to be in complete denial about the way the Universe works through its lesson plans.

Once you learn this then you will see each person as is—a unique individual on a personal journey. There won't be any more comparison dilemma in your house, not since you've had to deal with family and friends and their dysfunctions.

The issue with lambasting or judging is that it could be detrimental to your relationship. When you start saying, "My ex-boyfriend would have taken out the trash," or "My ex-girlfriend used to give me back rubs after a long day," you're asking for an argument that you won't win. Instead of comparing, just tell your partner what you want and what is making you unhappy.

So, let the ex go and look at your partner with a new set of eyes so that you don't miss new opportunities. If this sounds like your situation, then you may not be ready. You might need to work on removing your heart from your previous relationship so that you can concentrate on the new one. I've already told you that the heart is in charge, if you let it. No one wants to be the ball caught on a rebound.

If you're not ready to share your heart with anyone else, then take a time out. Why bring an innocent person into that half-filled cup? Maybe it's time that you are honest with yourself too. Why are you frequently thinking about your ex? Do you have regrets? Are you secretly wishing that you could be with your ex rather than your current partner? An honest answer to these questions will help you focus on the present or make a U-turn.

If your ex is bringing you drama and seems to want to hold on to a relationship that has long terminated, then stand up to the situation. Work through that problem by putting it, including the ex, in its proper place.

Don't allow your ex to bombard your relationship energy with negativity, which has nothing to do with you. Remember that very rarely will a relationship end in happiness. Even the one who was suffering the most will still feel sadness at the end. So if you're getting constant phone calls, e-mails, and other attacks that cause you great distress, then you need to cut that link. Whatever that link is that's allowing that person to get to you.

If you don't have a child, then this should be very simple. However, if you do have a child together, then take time out to tell yourself that whatever madness this ex is hurling your way has nothing to do with you. Your ex is drowning in misery but is in desperate need of company that you don't want to keep anymore. Eventually, when your ex realizes that the arrows aren't hitting the bull's eye—which is you, your beautiful smile, and new life—then your ex must retreat. Take a deep breath and cut your ex loose.

Chapter 8

WHO NEEDS MONEY?

HOW FINANCIALLY SECURE is your partner? Do you have an inkling of an idea? Let's not forget that you have been to almost every restaurant, theater, and social scene in town, but for some reason, finances were never a part of the conversations. You two have only been satisfying the external appeasement of your desires.

Well, I'm here to say it's time to have that talk if you're in a serious relationship and have been conversing about marriage and children. I, for one, can't believe that we haven't gotten the message about finances, which, like communication, keep coming up as one of the causes of demise in relationships.

Although usually a third fiddler, finances are pivotal to the vitality of your relationship.

Does your soul mate need money?

"Since the 1970s, we've had this idea of marriage being about a soul mate," said Bradford Wilcox, director of The National Marriage Project at the University of Virginia, "(but) beneath that idea there's still this idea, for most people, that money matters in sort of guiding and sustaining a marriage" (Linn 2012).

Yes, you will have people who'll say that a person's debt and credit are irrelevant. Then why does it keep coming up? Read my words carefully: it might not matter right now because you're only dating! The moment that you say *I do* and start to have children, trust and believe FINANCES will come up, especially if there's a lack thereof. Your partner won't be able to conceal it from you because it will have a direct effect on what you can do.

Where do you stand financially?

Let's be for real, since you can't be any other way when talking about el dinero. Money is a necessity for survival in the world that we live in. Without it, you can't pay your bills (to supplement your daily necessities), your rent or mortgage (for that roof that keeps you comfortable and warm), and you can't buy food (to have the strength to live another day). We live in a hemisphere where it's not love that makes the world go 'round, but, unnaturally and precariously, it's that dollar bill.

Whether it makes or breaks your relationship once you know the details is a personal preference. Learn about the money matters now while you're dating so that you can go into this marriage with an honest viewpoint when it comes to any monetary issues. You may not want to live from PTP or be with someone who is knee deep in debt. So being informed is critical. Once told, you cannot explode later and say you weren't shown the crystal ball, which did not show money falling off the trees.

Those "dead presidents" are ruling our lives even when we would prefer otherwise. So, for that reason, it matters. And those who can't afford to pay their bills end up where? Now you're getting it! This isn't about having money define your relationship. It's about knowing that you'll have to either work a little harder with your partner or that your darling is good until the next major investment together, such as a house, another car, etc.

Once you start having children, the expenses will skyrocket. It was reported in a CNNMoney article that the cost to raise a child born in 2015 until 18 years old could be as high as a quarter of a million dollars, not including college (Vasel 2017). It doesn't look like mercy will come calling anytime soon because the costs keep increasing. Heck, the spike does not only affect raising children—the cost of food, gas, and other commodities has been fluctuating globally. You can name the reasons as well as anyone else, so be realistic about your financial situation.

Work it out from the beginning and have a plan if either one of you is in debt. What matters now is to reduce and eliminate. If your partner spends mindlessly, that's a red flag to be addressed immediately. Spending money that you don't have is like creating a pseudo sense of "I have" when in actuality, you "have not" but have just borrowed with interest.

It's a great feeling when you know that your net income will not have parentheses protecting it.

Save yourself from bickering about finances later on and talk about where you stand—and be frank about it. It's not time to pretend or live in fantasyland as Mr. Bezos, Mr. Gates, Ms. Winfrey, or Ms. Alakija.

Ladies and gentlemen, learn to control the impulsive and sometimes stress-release shopping habits. After numerous fights and frustrations, your partner will not be happy if you're the one spending like you have no sense, and now must work overtime just to keep up with all the other bills (even if you have an income). Likewise, snap out of it and stop flossing like you got it when you know you don't. For some, that's a Usain Bolt to divorce lane when your partner starts to see the real you.

Financial Crises: Good-Bye, Darling

Remember, many are not willing to accept the lack. Again, we all have our own preferences in life. It's not about right or wrong. It's a matter of what the person is willing to put up with. Money issues yield great stress, unhappiness, depression, anger, and resentment. Let go of the thought, "My baby will be by my side no matter what if it's true love." Such a statement only applies when you tell the truth from the beginning.

Some people are realistic when it comes to finances. They want to choose for themselves whether they want to put up with your spending habits or sprint to Breakup Ville. You need to let it be a choice. Don't trap the person because there will be much antipathy later if you're financially living under false pretense.

Many people might agree that money is not the most important thing in life. I got a grasp of this after the death of my bird and my male cousin a month apart. I got sick and felt depressed for about three months. Yet, my money in the bank could not save me from the billow that nearly swallowed me whole. But we must still earn a living.

After writing this section, an acquaintance asked me why finances are a deal breaker for some couples. Have you ever thought about that? Well, there are four possible answers to this question.

The first case is where you have a person who "grew up without." As a child, this person saw Mom and Dad struggle and had to live with second-hand clothes or hand-me-downs and rarely received what was asked. Actually, asking was out of the equation because it was apparent that Mom and Dad didn't have any extra money—ever.

These individuals sometimes promise themselves that they will never struggle the way their parents did. They cannot fathom why others complain about work. They are just content to have a job and be able to pay their bills. That's more important to them, not how satisfied they are with work.

So they bring that same mentality to their marriage. Paying the bills and having extra money are top priorities. They don't want their children to go through what they experienced in their youth. They might not even want to spend too much money because saving is a top

Mission Statement. They must have a nest egg for more rainy days even if they already have years' worth in savings. So, if you lose your job or your business is struggling, baby, you had better have plan B and C or else you're in deep trouble.

On the other hand, you have case number two: the people who "always had." They are what I call the Fendi-Gucci kind. These individuals have never seen a day of financial struggle in their lives. Whatever they wanted, they got from Mommy and Daddy. So as adults, they expect the same lifestyle. This means never having to fret about money. They are so overindulged that it's as if their whole world is collapsing if the funds are dwindling.

If they have to worry about paying the next bill or can't get what they want, which is new to them, then discontentment quickly settles in. Just as swiftly, they will decide that this is not the life that they wanted. So, they may move on to the next person who writes the checks and clearly has more money than you do. This is partially why the rich will rarely marry a vagrant who has no money. It not only causes friction, but also it's just understood that people who are on the same lane or close to that will understand your world better.

Then there's the third well-known case: the people who like to "keep up with the Joneses." These individuals base their life values highly on being able to keep up appearances and match or out-do their neighbors, family, and friends. Sometimes they simply refuse to live within their means or accept their current financial state. They would rather have 10 credit cards at their disposal to keep up with the façade than show that they have less than others. Marrying someone like this is quite challenging. If your financial situation changes, then you better be ready to get back on the country club or risk losing your spouse.

These Hyacinth-type partners are quick to say, "Well, Kate's husband surprised her with a 2019 BMW i8 Roadster and a couple's retreat in Sydney. What am I supposed to do with a box of chocolate and a dozen roses?" Oh, and don't get her started on what else you're not doing right because her friends are not struggling and don't ever have to ask about the price.

The fourth one is created by either partner. This is when a spouse doesn't handle financial responsibilities with reservation. This person squanders every paycheck and doesn't save or invest for retirement. This major problem brings frequent arguments and lots of gray hair. Imagine how upsetting it is to be of age to retire but then have very little due to your living-larger-than-life partner!

It's hard to satisfy these types of people if you're struggling because they see finances through their own customized lenses. If you're not banking like you used to, then you had better go get another J-O-B, open a business, or something. Their sense of financial success is based on never having to worry about money.

Does your partner belong in one of these groups?

Face Your Financial Reality

It's important to put your financial house in order because you can't escape it. Remember to discuss and be honest about where you stand financially. It will save you from having to cool an angry spouse later on.

Leave the door open when it comes to financial discussions. Imagine a husband that suddenly has a fatal heart attack, leaving his wife with three children. But since he used to take care of all the financial decisions, she's left frozen in place because she doesn't know where to start. Don't live in the dark when it comes to finances. Most importantly, support each other when it comes to money because, at the end of the day, it matters.

Many of us get into financial trouble because we refuse to face our financial reality. The credit card bills, the utility bills, the car note, and the long receipt on the organizer shows us where we stand, but sometimes we turn a blind eye. Or other times we do take the time to look at our debt but don't have the slightest clue how to get out of it. That's when we should consider getting external help or read up on how to eliminate debt. Maybe it's time to open that business you've been thinking about since you were 10 years old.

You will free yourself from stress the moment that you decide to face your financial reality. Stop those debt collectors from blowing up your phone once and for all. Better that you know where you stand than walk around pretending that your debt doesn't exist.

Chapter 9

CRIMINAL MINDS—STICKING UP YOUR FUTURE!

THIS ONE JUST crept up on me: Criminal past. It was not part of the brainstorm, but it's coming up for a reason. I'm just letting the mind dictate.

Some of you might be thinking, "Well, my partner does not have a criminal mind, so I can skip this," but let me tell you something, we don't always know our partner as well as we think. Anyone can have a sketchy past.

The United States locks up more people per capita than any other nation…There are 2.3 million people in confinement (Wagner and Sawyer 2018). Sadly, recidivism is a major concern for many families as many of these people find themselves back in confinement within years. Some people look for "familial love" from friends or the "cool" gangs who seemed to have it all: the cash, the newest cars, and the decked out house. Many young people finally feel like they are accepted and/or loved. They are confused about what to do with their lives and how to outgrow their environment.

If you have a record, especially a major felony, your partner has a right to know. Even if you don't spill the details, you should alert your partner that you were derailed sometime in the past. Yes, it's hard to talk about this chapter of your life but hopefully, you have since felt peace and have forgiven yourself for your old missteps.

Ultimately, it's about choice. Don't let that person find out from Google.com about you committing burglary, battery, or whatever after you have been together for years.

How did you forget about that when you were telling your partner about yourself? Why would you leave that out? Shame or not, you must open up and confide in your partner.

So if at some point while dating you find out more about this person on the Internet, then that's a sign to slow down and ask questions. For those of you who fall in this predicament, be honest, share with your partner what happened that made you take that life-altering route. You can't wear a ski mask forever. Let your partner see and feel that you were young and thoughtless, but now you are more mature and grounded. Then it's up to that individual to decide what to do with that information. If you are worried that part of your biography might not be accepted, then you have someone who can't take you with all that you bring with you.

Again, like the financial situation, this is also about a person's preference.

Google Me Not

The problem you encounter by keeping your criminal past hidden is losing your partner's trust. Your partner will wonder what other secrets you're hiding. Remember, you can taint a person's trust from just one lie, especially if it's a major one.

Who you were has a direct correlation to who you are today, for better or for worse. You may be a more accommodating man or woman now because you know what happened the last time you lost your cool. You don't want to go back there, in that warp. If you're trying to keep yourself under control, then why wouldn't that be important?

This could be serious if you are a sex offender or murderer. Who wants to unknowingly live with one? Hello, we need to protect ourselves and our children! Personally, I want to make the choice and not have him look me in the eye, knowing that I think he's someone he's not. It is vital that your partner knows about your criminal past, not only because of trust and fairness but because of how your history could deny you certain privileges that could affect that person as well. When you need to do anything that requires a criminal background check, do you really want your partner staring at you in public with that you-need-to-explain-yourself look?

Imagine the shock when your partner decides to google your name and what comes up is your full name under a website that lists felons. After clicking on that link, your picture—yes, that's your mugshot staring back at your partner—pops up with a BUSTED! sign across the frame. Imagine the feeling of betrayal to find out about your past activities this way.

Some of you might have heard about the man who hijacked the plane in New Jersey in 1972 but wasn't caught until 41 years later in Africa. This man changed his name, married, and had children but hid his true identity. Now, can you imagine waking up one day to find out that the man whom you have trusted, loved, slept next to for 40-plus years is not who he says he is? He was not only a robber but also a murderer.

Moments like these make me think about the importance of a full background check. I know that we don't think about it for our partner unless our dad or mom is in law enforcement. We laugh when we see movies like *Meet the Parents*, but in reality, I would not blame anyone who insists on a criminal background check for their potential wife/husband.

So do what you feel is right for your own peace of mind. Throw in criminal history when you have those table talks. It can't hurt to know who you're dealing with. You don't want to be caught off guard.

Yes, it might be true that few women, or men for that matter, will want to be with a notorious murderer for the obvious reasons, but then again that's the consequence of one's past and choices made. It's not fair to think that your partner should just shut out that part of your history. It's best that you get their reaction earlier on than wait until after marriage. At least then, your partner will understand whom they choose to marry because they love you and want to be with you despite your criminal past. Maybe only 1 out of 500 will accept you with that rap sheet, but at least you will have a sense of peace with that one.

Criminal Deeds: No Mercy

Oddly enough, after writing this section, it hit home like a brick. I had a relative who allegedly committed the worst crime imaginable. God knows what kind of identity he might take. After all, he allegedly took his own first cousin's life.

I often think of how he is doing mentally. A double tragedy indeed!

Understandably, it may be difficult to tell others about one's criminal past, but if you want to have an honest, free, and loving relationship, you cannot let it be hidden forever. You must be ready for whichever way your partner responds. If it's not communicated, it will eat you up inside like a flesh-eating disease, and that's not fair to your relationship.

Sometimes we commit a foul without thinking of the consequences. We forget to think that what we do today could cripple us tomorrow. And to have a criminal rap sheet, especially serious offenses, is a form of paralysis. Despite those later pains, some people commit crimes because it gives them an abnormal sense of high and power over their victims. Or it could be because Mom or Dad brought some of that activity home and so it's almost normal to them. Why work hard when you can just take it from the vulnerable? But then the table turns because later on, they usually end up giving up their freedom.

Thieves broke into my apartment one day before Valentine's Day 2012, the same day my young female cousin was buried. It was disturbing to see my clothes on the floor, drawers pulled out, and purses emptied. However, I was lucky not to have lost so much as a pen. Just the thought of a stranger in my space, uninvited, ravaging through my personal belongings truly offended me. I've been a victim of criminal minds a few times but nothing life-threatening. I didn't live in dangerous neighborhoods, but I still couldn't escape people with sticky fingers. So, we do live in a world where some people have no respect for others' properties, or even life itself. We can't be too vigilant in protecting ourselves.

I come from a line of people that will shun you if you have a criminal past. They think of it as sullying the family name or destroying the dignity and respect of your relatives through the eyes of your neighbors. They don't waver in their sentiments one bit. Since I didn't grow up around neighborly distrust, I didn't think about one's criminal past. It wasn't a natural thought for me. That might be the same case for you as well. However, an unexpected experience might make you reconsider.

Do you know of all that you will experience before you leave this Earth?

Well then, think of this. After about one year of dating, you learned that your significant other was a felon thanks to playing around on Google.com one night. You suddenly felt bemused and betrayed by what you saw. Because this never came up, despite your deep conversations about both of your pasts. Would you have felt differently if you were told? Absolutely! At least then you would know that you made the choice to be with someone who is limited in many ways.

I had met a guy whom I never thought of as a felon until his restrictions started to prevent him from partaking in the simple things. However, I must say that it does have its challenges when you decide to accept that person "as is" at the present. I figured that was the Universe's way of teaching me something different. I'm not talking about a minor felony nor am I talking about murder, but still, the crime was a major enough offense in the eyes of the law.

Part of his criminal past and lack of self-love, confidence, and emotional connection stemming from childhood were a huge suction to the strength of the relationship. But then, I thought he was not the same young man who'd made those immature choices and I believed he really changed. But the change appeared superficial, as his heart was still shattered, suspicious, angry, and sadly, one of the invisible parasites that sped up the end of our relationship. His criminal past combined with a damaging childhood turned his, and subsequently my, world upside down.

Again, there I was trying to rehab a grown man who didn't even understand himself. In the end, I had to choose between being happy, raising my eldest son in a healthy environment, or continuing to be with a man who was walking around with the Underworld on his shoulder.

Yes, we all make mistakes in life. I've made too many to count. There's not one person who could honestly tell me that they have lived a perfect life, not even the ones whom we hold to an angelic height. A perfect life is one where you have no obstacles to overcome. We know that eventually, anyone who walks this Earth will face them. But how we overcome and when we acknowledge our mistakes is the key, especially for people with a criminal past. Talking to the person you want to marry one day about it is certainly no small or unnecessary feat. It's mandatory!

Chapter 10

NO CAVIAR

NO, THIS IS not about sushi. It's still about your future. When this title came up, I didn't immediately realize how it paralleled with the rest of this section until I read an article, days later, discussing what people from different countries eat on New Year's Day. Some people think fish symbolize abundance since they swim in schools.

So the key point here is simple: Do not let too many issues crowd or overwhelm you. This is not the kind of abundance you want. When you meet the love of your life, surely, you picture how life will be between you two. But what do you see?

What you survey through that constricted tunnel are usually only the good things. People rarely think about the other subsets of life where things could go wrong. It's like life and death. Death is as much a part of our experience as life, yet few people plan for or accept that earthly reality. When you think you've met your match, you have to look at the overall scheme of things. You must be prepared for the good and the bad of merging two lives. Ready or not, life will have its way.

You have to look at your partner to see if this person is someone you can spend your life without. No, it doesn't literally mean that you can't survive without that person, although, it is true that sometimes when you lose a dear one, you're never quite the same. I had a cousin who was only in his early thirties when he transitioned. His bereft widow still hasn't remarried 26 years later. When you have experienced true love and lived like twin flames, it's hard to deal with some of the knuckleheads who come knocking.

I was extremely surprised at how much I enjoyed the stage play on DVD, *What My Husband Doesn't Know*, written, directed, and produced by David E. Talbert, starring Michelle Williams from Destiny's Child, Brian White, and Clifton Duncan. One of the lines that stuck with me came from Franklin, Lena's millionaire construction mogul husband, when he said he looked for a woman he couldn't live without, unlike most men (2012).

Who are these types of men or women?

They build you up when you are in despair. They make you smile when you are sad. They massage your feet or rub your back after a long day's work. They take care of your normal responsibilities because you are burned out. They are happy when you get home and are ready to hear about your day. They know when to give you breathing room. And they know when to pull you close and give you a bear hug.

Commonalities

Ask yourself these questions: What does my partner want from life? Are our values and principles similar or do they clash? How do I want my life to be when I marry?

I can give you the dictionary definition of values, but we will keep it simple. Your values are what guide you in times of decision making. They are never far away to steer you on the right path, your own path, when you need directions. So if those beliefs, and things that are of great importance to you, are looked upon as trivial or meaningless by your partner, you need to think seriously about that. The decisions that we make in life depend on those principles and values. So examine your partner's reaction to your Ps & Vs, especially if this person derisively dismisses them as invaluable.

I think this could also be thought of along the same line as your faith or conviction. What are your religious or spiritual beliefs? For example, when I interviewed the couple who has been married for 20 years, I could tell right away that their religious faith had a major impact on how they viewed their marriage and what they needed to make it last. That was key to them. Their similar beliefs help them create a more peaceful home, and it can be felt in the energy around them and their house.

You don't have to be religious to have conviction, but whatever your beliefs, it helps when both partners have a bigger picture in mind. Having common values helps because we live in a world where diversity is still an issue, as if there's only one way. If that were so, then none of us would make it when it came time to receive our reward. How simple life would be!

It makes a big difference to meet like-minded people, or people who accept you despite your different beliefs. Whatever path you take, whether religious or spiritual, keep that in mind. You don't want your wonderful relationship to turn into something detestable.

Unfortunately, everyone is not as accepting of others, which is one reason our beautiful planet is falling apart. You must find that common thing in your partner that you can rely on during the hard times. It could be something as simple as your love to travel, cook, or watch classical movies together. Look at any long-lasting relationship and you will find this to be true.

I Want To Ask You Something

As your relationship gets serious, you must ask questions along the way. Does your partner want to have children or even be monogamous? What type of lifestyle is preferred? Does it conflict with how you want to live? Don't wait until after you are husband and wife to try to figure each other out. What you two need to learn as a couple should be how to become one now, before you're married. Don't ask, "Who is that stranger that I just gave the key to my heart?" Don't assume that everyone wants that white picket fence, with two children, and a pet.

Now is the right time to start analyzing what your partner has shown you over the period of your courtship.

Here's another shocker: Not everyone believes in commitment. Don't be too quick to assume that marriage equates to loyalty or fidelity. Nope, I dare say that there are many men and women who get married but aren't ready to or don't want to give themselves to just one person. Some think the idea is illogical. They know that they will yearn for la nouvelle belle or le nouveau beau once things start to feel too redundant. It's not about you or about how you feel about that. So don't be shy; ask whether or not your partner wants to be in a committed relationship. The answer might shock you.

Although marriage is believed to be sacrosanct, not everyone defines it that way. Both parties must see it as sacred or else you will have relationship schism.

More questions to ponder about over the course of your courtship: What are this person's dreams and aspirations? Are they similar to yours?

I dream of a life where I have peace, love, and support from my spouse. I want a man who can appreciate me as I AM and who is there to help me progress and learn how to decode this life. I want to be able to speak my mind, to carry intelligent but sometimes simple conversations, to learn new things, and to be treated with respect like the special woman that I AM. Meeting and loving such a man who understands that is important to me. It doesn't mean that I expect my life to be all-happy all the time. God knows that I'm too complicated for that. Actually, women are complicated, yet we're simple once understood. Like life, we are a paradox. Our lives are full of twists and turns.

To know that we are a paradox should propel us to get to know our partners on a deeper level. Leave out the assumptions, which will do nothing but cause more frustration. It's impossible to know someone well unless you ask questions.

The Ascended Visual

I have met many people who do not dream at all. That is, they are mechanistically letting life lead without taking control over how they want their lives to be. They lack what I call *the ascended visual*. This is the picture you see in your mind's eye, the one you can tweak when necessary. Whatever is on that picture is what you put on it. It's all yours!

Once you are aware of this, nothing will ever be the same again. Noticing it is like getting a dose of the Energizer Bunny of ambition and hope. So when you communicate your dreams, pay attention to how they are perceived. Does your significant other laugh at your dreams? You may not get the support you need later to fulfill them. And that, my friend, is a sign of division, which could later lead to divorce.

Based on a true story: a young man had big dreams, and one of them was to be an entrepreneur. But his wife didn't agree with how he wanted to accomplish his visions, which crushed his spirit. So he eventually looked for that support elsewhere, and it pained him that his wife wasn't that bridge.

But because he was so lost from the beginning and not allowed to use all the necessary resources to make it flourish, his entrepreneurial dream became a nightmare. He not only lost that dream, but his mother's soul saluted the heavens too soon to witness him succeed in life.

His non-supportive wife did not care enough about his dreams, his family, or his values. Even after this tragedy, nothing changed as he continued to walk around with his mind trapped in the basement. The interesting thing is, he had the signs while they were dating, but how many of us look at those red flags and blame our lack of attentiveness on the notion that love is blind?

If you get nothing else from this book, remember not to give up on your dreams just so that you can be in a relationship with someone who doesn't care about your happiness. You may regret it later.

Cate Blanchett, who played Katharine Hepburn in the movie, *The Aviator,* said it best when she exclaimed to Leonardo DiCaprio, who played Howard Hughes, that she had met someone who was more attuned to her needs (Scorsese 2004). That's exactly the type of person you need to make your relationship work when you're married, a person who is attuned to your needs.

Figuring out your purpose is just as important as breathing to have a meaningful life and marriage. You may not get everything that you want in one lifetime, but there's nothing wrong with aspiring to a greater existence full of positive attributes, love, sharing, and learning. If the person you're with wants to just be a drifter, then you have a long road ahead of you. If you want much more out of life, you're setting yourself up for disappointment. You can talk this out to see if this person is willing to see where you're coming from.

Remember that you can't expect your partner to always want the same as you, but don't let that stop you from speaking up about what matters to you. You should leave room for compromising, though, as long as it's realistic and you aren't crushing your dreams; nary a one. You cannot be the only one with a plan, or else you will be the only one working toward it. After all, it's your plan. Your boyfriend never told you that he wanted a house, a career, or to be free of debt. Your girlfriend never declared that she wanted to have children, stop hanging out with her girlfriends, or be a career woman.

With one-sided plans come stress, resentment, and, well, more reasons to be unhappy and divisive. You both must want to eat, or at least sample, the caviar of life for your marriage to have an abundance of the best. Remember to communicate your goals, ask questions, and listen well. Never assume anything!

PART TWO

Chapter 11

BEFORE THE BIG HOOPLA

BEFORE YOU START accepting or planning that super-romantic proposal or your big day, you have some chores to do. What I would like to call a little housekeeping or tareas domesticas.

Here are some of the things that you should accomplish or at least consider before you finally decide that you want to be Mr. and Mrs. Compatible. As with all the other ideas in this book, these tasks are for both men and women. Of course, the list is general and limited, but you can add your own ideas to it. In fact, you should!

Ask yourself, "What is it that I need to do for myself before that big passage?"

Foremost, you need to understand diversity and spirituality to deal with the differences that you will encounter from your soon-to-be spouse. That's what is missing in many households. It's missing from a majority of relationship books. It's missing from most table talks. Getting right to it, for your marriage to last longer, you both need to go back to being spiritual beings, not necessarily religious, but spiritual, because there's a difference. I shouldn't have to remind you that you could be super religious and yet be spirituality dormant because you don't have internal peace.

I might lose some of you here for a minute, so hold onto your seats and open your minds and hearts. This is not an attack on any particular religious organization or belief system, but let me take you to primordial church for a second.

To save your marriage, I'm challenging you to take a spiritual journey before the wedding. The reason? Marriage is cosmic and spiritual, so you must be prepared for it. You must let go of the ego and be ready to connect with your spouse on a higher plateau.

Spiritual Journey: Save Yourself

A spiritual journey is about acceptance of self and others. We need to go through it, and when we let go, the noises of self-destruction will cease. During my journey, I met all types of people. Some were helpful, but many were not so stellar. I learned that just because someone was saying Namaste or teaching about spirituality didn't mean that they live exemplary lives. Some of these people are actually shady and manipulative. So, beware!

Eventually, I had to go deep within myself and limit how much I received from others. I had to fight and work with what was keeping me from having a long-lasting relationship and what was attracting certain types of men into my life. I had to go back to primordial church and undo the damage caused by some of my childhood experiences.

Now, it's your time to go back to that church. It's not a religious place, but instead, it's a state of mind. It is spiritual. You'll be surprised to learn that your spirituality has very little to do with other people. Even if you meet someone who is instrumental while on your journey, in order to connect with it, you must still go within first. No one can go on the journey for you.

You can be overtly religious and fool many, including yourself, but you cannot dismiss spirituality because it and you are one. No matter what you put out there, deep down on the inside, you intrinsically know the real deal. What goes on internally doesn't always align with what you show externally, which is what others see and judge.

The word spirit comes from the Latin word *spiritus* or *spirare,* and it means *breath* or *to breathe.* My insight is that it's more than just breath. How and where does spirit manifest? On Earth, it's described as a vital force *within* animated beings. It actually manifests within as well as outside of us. Our spirit doesn't dwell in us, and it doesn't need our body for it to be. In order to function on this material plane, it takes on the form of breath. It's not a new revelation that we're primarily of spirit. That spark which gives us consciousness. We're able to be who we are on this Earth because of it. Bring your attention to the voice in your head for a second. How can you disconnect from that which is an inseparable part of you?

The spirit within us doesn't care whether we believe in the Trine, or Trinity, or if we're religious; it simply does its job to keep us alive. It's the root word in spirituality, and that's not by coincidence! You might have a devout, well-versed, always-at-Sunday-service person be more sinister than one who stays to self and does more good in the community and at home. Spirituality does not need a moderator telling you who is your brother or sister because deep down we are one. It does not need a crowd of sameness because, again, it understands the variance of this Universe.

According to *The Compact Guide to World Religions*, there are 12 major religions in the world. How many can you name besides your own and the most common? They are as follows: Christianity, Judaism, Hinduism, Buddhism, Islam, Baha'i, Zoroastrianism, Jainism, Sikhism, Confucianism, Shinto, and Taoism (O'Callaghan 2010). But in Mother Nature's book, of which you are a co-creator, there's incredibly only one spirituality but many spirits. Despite how divisive we are as a human race, once we accept our spirituality, it will always take us back to the Source.

Close your eyes for a second, and without thinking of what you were taught, answer these questions: What is life? Why are you here? Why, and how, do you know what you know? What is beyond this realm?

Maybe you can't answer these questions with certainty, and that's understandable. To the human mind, even the absolute is relative. Being spiritual drives you not only to love yourself but also to have more tolerance of the diversity on this planet. While religion should be the principal here, we know that a few controlling groups have turned that subjective connection into something secluded and exclusive.

On the other hand, spirituality, that light that is in every living thing, will make us understand that LIFE is quite majestic in all its mysteries and paradoxical episodes. We started out the same way, even if we eventually look, feel, and sense things in our own personal experience. But ultimately, the variations of our inevitable journeys are very connected. The Universe manifests in each of us in different ways. Every living and non-living thing exhibits the multiple facets of The Higher or what some would call God, Allah, YHVH or Jehovah, Krishna, Mungu, or Elohim. If you could think of people as mini-Gods, since many of us believe that we were created in His and Her image, then it will be much easier for you to embrace your spirituality, and that of others.

When we realize this, especially as humans, then we will be free of the ignorance that's at the core of our potential demise as a loving people. We will then realize that we embody each other's energies, and at the end, to harm another being, or to abuse that which is alien to us, is to cause great harm to ourselves. You are me, and I am you. No one is better than you, for we're part of the same experience. We're carrying a unique torch, but for the same team, a part of the beginning and the end, the Alpha and the Omega. Who are you to extinguish that light? Who am I? We are the same, but in multiples, to the Universe.

We live, we experience, and then we transition. Tell me of one who doesn't transition or transform? I couldn't have put it any better than the Dalai Lama, who has wisely stated many times that we are one Earth community. When we make that connection with the Universe, our eyes will be opened to the bottom line. Then we'll learn to calm ourselves down, take better care of ourselves, and treat each other with love and utmost respect. And of course, cherish the blessed moments with our partner.

We're taking part in something that even the genius of the geniuses can't fully decipher and explain. Some of you might be scratching your heads, or some might feel offended, but that's not my aim. I'm not asking you to stop going to church or to give up your religion; that's your personal business. These institutions have helped a lot of people deal with their issues or feel like they have a purpose, which is good for them.

Religion in itself is not a bad thing as long as you aren't being programmed, controlled, or manipulated into giving up your powers. However, I want to remind you not to leave your spirituality at the door. Not only does your happiness depend on it, but also your marriage will thank you profusely.

Accepting and loving your partner, with their differences, are fundamental to the spiritual state of your union. It doesn't mean we will always accept or like everybody's ways, but guess what—you just have to find the one somebody who will accept you as you are.

RED ALERT: We should work through our differences, but not at the cost of our peace of mind and love of self. That comes first! We can accept differences, but we can't accept negativity every day of the week if it's stifling our growth. There are people who haven't heard from me in years for that same reason. I don't like to wallow in confusion and chaos for long. I'm a problem-solver, which causes me to give too much of myself sometimes. But I can't be with a man who's about nothing yet expects that I will continue to take care of him and his needs daily. Where's the help?

Be aware of those differences and determine the ones you can and cannot deal with. Those will be the ones that will lead to divorce if left unchecked. I know it's a challenge. However, once recognized, you must either resolve or turn away, instead of making it worse by attacking.

When you're spiritual, you will be at peace with yourself and others, even the ones who irk you and those you have to let go. Your life will never be the same again. You won't be so tempted to bring all of that mundane and unproductive energy into your home. It will be easier for you to understand your partner because you won't think like everyone else. You won't have so many excuses, but rather you'll see your problems as temporary and that you hold the key to your own happiness. And that's exactly what a marriage needs: to have serenity and spiritual unity in order to handle your business, especially during those frustrating moments. If you haven't already, start thinking about that spiritual journey. Meditate on it. The journey is definitely worth it.

NOW   **IF...**

- it feels awkward when you're together
- you don't truly love your partner
- you are lost and confused about what you want in life
- you are not happy when you think of your relationship
- you are only attracted to their body, good looks, or money
- you know you're gay or lesbian but are pretending to be otherwise to please others
- you don't know your partner that well
- you are always eager to end your rendezvous
- you feel no excitement when together
- you don't complement and balance each other
- you want vastly different things in life
- you have trust issues, either of self or of partner
- you are marrying out of obligation
- you don't want to get married

Chapter 12

PASTORAL COUNSELING

YOU ARE THE driver on your journey, although you will get plenty of help along the way. The ride may not always be pleasant, but it can be thrilling.

Before I got married, the pastor wanted my ex-husband and me to do two weeks of counseling. Our dilemma? We didn't have two weeks since my ex had just joined the military and we wanted to wed before he left. We went to pastoral counseling for one day, and I remember him asking many questions. Anyhow, we knew that we were ready to tie the knot, and I was soon to join my husband in Europe after the school semester was over.

The pastor looked at me and with a teasing smile said, "That's one strong woman you have there! Even though she's not saying much, she's something else."

I was a burnt-out sophomore at Montclair State University while attending Army ROTC at Seton Hall University. Never once did I envision myself as a divorced single mom during my engagement months. But deep down even before the wedding, I had some doubts.

The night my ex-husband proposed to me, we'd had a big fight on our way home because he'd left me waiting for more than one hour in the cold at the university campus. I was even more upset that he was driving my car with his BFF in the passenger seat. I was fuming, to say the least. I'm told that she's now his wife, and I wish them nothing but the best. I know I missed so many signs, but I'm not angry. I was too inexperienced to see them. I didn't say yes when he proposed. It took me several weeks to mull it over. We married nearly a year after that and divorced five years later.

Pastoral counseling can only scratch the surface, so be honest with yourself. Is this really what you want to do? Are you truly ready to share your everyday life with someone else?

For many of us, that part of the marriage is a problem, especially when the man or woman we married turns into an ugly, suffocating leech. This is when it counts to have more than just the superficial in common. The vows to one another is a major decision, although, many of us take it for granted. Divorce stings! It's not easy to have a connection with your ex and deal with some of the BS. And some exes make it hell!

So, although pastoral counseling or any type of couple counseling is not a guarantee that your relationship will last, it can at least get you thinking of whether or not you're ready for this major commitment; however, you'll be the master of the results. You're the principal of your *dharma*. You're the Overseer!

If before, during, or after counseling you hear that little voice questioning your engagement and you have uneasy butterflies in your stomach, pay attention!

These doubts will accelerate your intolerance to deal with those marital problems that are a part of being a couple. Be conscious of your feelings now, before marriage. It's critical that you do your homework and be aware of your emotions. If what you're feeling is not genuine joy and love, then stop now.

Whose Wedding Is It?

Don't let other people make this decision for you. Not your pastor, not your parents, nor your friends. Yes, they can have an opinion about your relationship and share their concerns, but the route you take should be your own.

Much of what we experience in life is culturally based. For instance, I have heard of, and even seen, many African movies where the parents are very involved in their children's dating life. I have much respect for African producers, writers, and the African culture. I'm in love with their movies and music! Although movies are usually fantasies recreated, there are cultural essences that come through in them. I have a few African acquaintances who confirm what I see in those interesting movies.

As a matter of fact, one of the ladies who does my hair tells me that although you get to choose your mate, in Africa, your parents' approval has much weight. This is one reason why the divorce rate is lower there, since Africans take their vows very seriously. It's frowned upon to marry unless your parents see that the man is responsible, stable, and capable of handling the challenges of marriage, and that the woman is ready to fulfill her wifely duties. This is especially true in the upper middle and upper class. I wondered about that for a second and thought that as long as the parents were not forcing their son or daughter to marry then there was no harm in that.

But parents should not go overboard, which to me is never a good thing. In my opinion, parents must not interfere too much in their children's adult lives. They can talk and share their insights, but should they have the last say? Who will wake up next to that person? Is it your mom, your dad, or you? So you had better be happy with the choice that YOU made.

Sometimes, we even feel pressured to marry. Your parents want grandchildren. You're getting older. Your friends are now married with children. You, on the other hand, are still single and you have not yet found The One. So what! Don't let that rush you into getting married when you aren't ready. And don't fall victim to "I got tired of being alone, so I wanted to marry." That's not a good enough reason to just race down the aisle.

The bottom line is that when you marry, it should be what you both want, and you should both be ready. Use pastoral counseling and other recommendations as a supplement, not as the glue that will make your marriage last. Use them only when you deem necessary. The glue should be your love and understanding of each other. You are each other's lock and key.

So again, whose wedding is it? If you've been asking yourself this same question, then acknowledge that you are making a mistake. If you have a headache whenever you think of walking down that aisle, then why make that walk. You already have the signs that there is a problem.

Chapter 13

I AM NOT

TO KNOW WHO you are is to recognize what, and who, you are not. I know about this tragedy firsthand. If you huddle a bunch of 17- to 21-year-olds and listen to them talk, you might believe that what they think of themselves and their lives is true because they have even convinced themselves. This isn't to say that you can't be young and know who you are, but it is not as likely, as we often need experience to understand ourselves better.

We have seen young prodigies who are as wise as elders. They act and talk like they have lived thousands of lives before this one. But for the rest of us, getting a glimpse of who we are comes with time and experience because most of us are dormant.

When I was 18 years old, I thought I knew what I wanted from life, and I thought I knew who I was. I'm bringing this up to say that when we're young our scope of life is limited. Many of us have been sheltered or only had a peek at what life is all about, or maybe what we know was projected on us.

Now, in my late 30s, I realize that I was nothing more than a walking robot. I used that phrase loosely in the past when referring to my late teens to early 20s, but now I see that it was true. Those days look like a long dream to me because I was in a dream state.

Case in point: By the time I was 18, I had a broken heart from my first love. I had a man twice my age who was crazy in love with me a few years before that. I suffered religious alienation from my own denomination because I didn't want to conform. I lost two close cousins in 1992 and 1999; bless their eternal souls. I was kicked out of my home, and then emancipated by my ex-husband and his best friend.

Can you say total chaos! Yet, I thought I knew what I was doing. I bet if you had asked me then who I was, I would have repeated what I was taught about myself. Who else can answer that question better than you? However, you will know more of yourself after you have gotten a taste of the real world.

It's great to have someone who's already self-aware, but it doesn't mean that you can't work with them if they're learning about themselves. It does take more energy and tolerance, but you can allow yourself to exit if that's what is best.

I'm a Capricorn, and if you've studied us, you know that we're persistent high-achievers, intuitive, and assertive. Although I've surpassed some of the Capricorn traits, deep down I still carry many of those same prominent characteristics of The Goat. When we love, we love hard and faithfully! You have to be on your A-game to deal with us. We expect our relationship to grow, and we can't deal with half-truths. We are very committed. We are doers and teachers, but we can also be as cold as ice. A guy doesn't want to have a Cappy grow cold because it means that we've completely extinguished the fire. It takes some time to get there, though, because we don't give up so easily. My advice: Don't take for granted the one that you love, especially when they reciprocate that sentiment.

I once sent the following text in response to a shared quote about how the mind gets angry but the heart always still cares. I said, "True, until the person you care about constantly batters and breaks the heart, and then it gradually becomes hardened until it stops caring. The heart can take but so much before it wakes up and becomes in sync with the mind. The heart is usually two steps behind the mind."

As we get older, our mind plays tricks on us. It challenges us to look inward to test ourselves and forces us to seek peace. The consequence? Well, either a divorce or patiently working with your partner to accommodate the new you. It's not easy, but let's work with the latter.

Even if others won't accept you as you are, you owe it to your sanity to love yourself, and be yourself as long as you're mentally and spiritually healthy. Give yourself carte blanche to do you!

Take your time. I cannot stress this enough. Time is important for any relationship to flourish. Use the time during your courtship to get to know who you are as well as who is standing next to you.

Embrace Yourself!

In time, you should also know some of your own strengths and weaknesses as an individual and as a partner. You'll continue to evolve in life, but you should work on yourself before you accept that magical proposal.

Primarily, be honest and true to yourself, study yourself, and know what will nourish your soul. Figure out what's important to you. Broaden your views about life, other people, and other cultures. Be kind to yourself. Have a conversation with your inner voice. I'm not saying for you to walk around talking to yourself, but do listen to what your mind and heart are telling you. Pick out the lies that you might be telling yourself about who you are.

Are you pretending to be your Aunt Vickie, your friend Tracy, or your Mama Dee? Are you keeping up with the Carters because you don't like the real you? Are you telling people what they want to hear about you just to appease them? Or are you saying, no matter what, you are the beautiful sentient being who is here on this Earth for a purpose, and to work to live a peaceful life by being at your humanly best?

You can see why being true to yourself and taking the time to know, love, and embrace yourself matters so much if you want to have a satisfying and complete marriage. This is not a sham. We live in a time when people are more concerned with and attentive to the outside world, celebrities, and other worldly distractions. Everything but themselves. We're like the prying neighbor who sits on the porch talking about every passerby yet forgets that one day that passerby will be them. This homework of self is not solely for you but also for your partner, your children, and the people you meet in life.

    I have experienced what not loving oneself does, especially to a man. Unfortunately, a lack of self-love and an underdeveloped sense of self creates chaos, not only for that man, but also for the girlfriends and the wives. A man who does not, or cannot, sense himself will not be able to carry the torch of sensing someone else. He will continue to be a tormented soul. Love yourself and learn about who you are.

Chapter 14

LINE IN THE SAND

LIFE IS FULL of challenges, contradictions, and paradigms. Trust me, when they say that you become one as husband and wife, this statement will amplify by folds.

The road of matrimony is challenging, especially now as the roles have evolved, and some people get confused over what they are supposed to do, or be, as man/husband and woman/wife. In certain households, the women are now the primary breadwinners. Men have to acknowledge that the days of being the sole decision maker are kaput. So both genders will have to put in extra effort to keep peace in their homes.

Now, I'm not saying to keep a tight grip on your spouse, as if this person is a commodity. In that case, the person who is being sucked into this vacuum will eventually stop responding and will go elsewhere for what is lacking at home. You can't be too domineering, yet you also can't be too naïve and carefree. What you need is a balanced attitude.

In any successful relationship, you must know what you will and won't tolerate. Yes, you won't always know how you'll react in each situation until such time presents, but we all have limits. Know and express yours. Don't wait until it is too late to do so. If someone constantly pushes your buttons, ask yourself if you told them not to.

For instance, my boundaries are unequivocally expressed in some way when I'm in a relationship: appreciation of quality time together, love for family, respect for self, and willingness to progress/mature. I want my life to be more than just time passing by.

Another major issue is that since I'm a mother, my "be sexy" time must be planned. I can't always go out on intimate date nights, and I don't make excuses for being a devoted mother. It doesn't mean that I have forgotten about myself as a woman. I know when to pull the plug and unwind. Nevertheless, raising my sons well and their well-being are my priorities until they're grown. When my sons chose me as their mom and I accepted to give birth to them, I made a silent commitment to raise them in a loving and supportive environment because we live in a crazy and sometimes dangerous time. If my partner supports me at home, then this won't even be an issue. However, if I'm overwhelmed, then my sexy time will definitely take a hit.

Yes, there's more! I have a strong bond with my dear mother. She's my main soul-sistah! My relationship with Ma Mère is off limits. I know who my partner is, but I'm also aware of the importance of my close relatives.

Now, the danger comes if I were to share more with others than with my partner. He would have to look at why that's the case. Is he pushing me away?

If I'm not taking away from our personal time, then there's nothing to be jealous about. We should let our partner breathe easy when it comes to familial relationships. Don't threaten them because they want to continue the existing bond with Mom, Dad, Brother, Sister, and old friends if they're not prying. Just because you are now a couple doesn't mean that your partner needs to stand solo.

This is serious because there have been too many men and women who spitefully prevent their lover from having a great relationship with the family. They will always be family. It doesn't mean that you must spend time with them if they are drama-fested, but keep in mind that it's important to be respectful of your spouse's interaction with their family. If the family is not interfering in your relationship, then back off.

Most people want a companion who is willing to compromise and share. Someone who knows that marital happiness comes from both partners. If your partner is keeping you from your family, friends, or those people who are important to you while you're dating, then you make that call. I'm not talking about keeping toxic people in your life.

Past experience has taught me it's best not to entertain drama. Both men and women lie, even to the one they love, when they can't think of a way to cool things. Don't let this escalate to the point where everyone loses touch with you if that's not what you want. Expect respect and give the same. Anyone who complains about this has some maturing to do. It's not about acting more important or feeding the ego. It's called respecting the one you love.

Yellow Light!

This section is in congruence with the other one that talks about knowing yourself first. That's why you must "share" for others to know you. Otherwise, what they think is only an assumption or a projection of what they perceive about you. To communicate your boundaries, you must know what you want and who you are. For example, you could meet someone with whom you seem to be incompatible in the beginning, but once you remove some of your pre-judgment and get to know and respect each other's boundaries then it could be a great match.

I don't know you personally, but I'll bet that you have boundaries. Some of them might be looked upon as silly and crazy, but you don't need approval from anyone to have them. Your partner will have certain quirks that could rub you the wrong way too. But know when it's time to bow out respectfully.

There are even people whose boundaries consist of their partner not consuming certain foods and not speaking improperly. What about not accepting a person who has no college degree! The list could be as long as this book.

Set and discuss your boundaries now if it appears that your partner has a problem with them. Whatever your boundaries, if they're important to you, then talk about them so that your partner know the meaning behind that look you give when something is bothering you.

Anything that your partner does that triggers a negative feeling is like a yellow light, warning you to work with that issue. You can run through it, thinking that you'll be all right in the end, or you can slow down and resolve it before it turns into a dis-ease. The boundaries are there to test you. They are a sign that you need to slow down.

Chapter 15

BE REALISTIC

DO ME A huge favor. Cliff off those reality shows and return to Earth with me for a second. I'm glad that people's interests in some of these shows are dwindling, even if just a little. Television can be a great tool, but sometimes it feeds us junk.

It seems we cannot differentiate between what's real and what's exaggerated for ratings, since our generation loves sex exploitation, drama, and vanity.

I'm not annoyed about people finding entertainment. But it's irritating to see how people forget about their own lives, get lost in these shows, and know more about these actors than they do about themselves or about what's going on in their households. Why don't you give your own life and your partner that much attention on schedule?

If you're like the rest of us, then it's time to get back to Earth. Remember that living in someone else's world can also doom your relationship if you don't know when to go back to your own reality.

Marriage is not going to be happy-happy every day. You will have moments during your marriage when you'll want to be left alone or will need to work through new developing issues. There will be no perfection, as both of you figure out this thing called life. Temptations may surface, but hopefully, they will be short-lived or fully eradicated. Your wife won't be waking up next to you with a perfect coif or always walking around in sexy lingerie. Yes, this will change, especially once you start having children, since then she will have to split her time between motherhood and wifehood, both of which can be very demanding. Know what you're getting into and whether this is the person you want to wake up next to daily, without the makeup and fancy clothes. There will be a time for sexy, but it might not be every time you see each other.

Reality Academy

Can you work through each other's quirks? Are you lowering your standards to say *I do*? It's easy to say that we can leave the guy who mistreats us or let go of the girl who has no sense, but it's not always that cut and dry. However, if you find yourself losing grip on who you are becoming just so that you can be in this relationship, then it's time to do a reality check.

You are both human beings with shortcomings. It will take much effort for your marriage to work. But it could be simpler if you make it that way. However, most of us prefer the hard road and then complain about why it has to be so difficult. Your marriage will be an act of yin and yang. That's the only way for your lives to be in sync. It's all about time, which is your new mutual best friend.

Time will put things in their proper place, heal and seal your bond, appreciation, and love for one another.

This is why you don't want to waste it, because once it's passed, it's gone. Be mindful of the present and your time together. When you look at your partner, can you forgive and live with the issues that bother you?

Love and marriage are beautiful no matter what's happening to prove them otherwise. You must be mature and ready to deal with your cards during your marriage. But your courtship is the pre-test that prepares you for those unrevealed hands. True, there will be more twists and turns that won't be so apparent. Nevertheless, if you're presently harmonious in the way the two of you work, then chances are you will be prepared to handle most of your marital issues.

Many people wonder why things change so much after marriage. It's possible that you were inseparable and in love while dating, but once married you started scratching your head wondering, "What the heck was I inhaling?" You must tell yourself NOW that you're in this for the long haul and not merely for the good times. Despite the melancholy news of how quickly people are getting divorced, your marriage does not have to be in that pool, if you follow through and become more aware of each other, now and as your relationship gets more serious.

If you're not being real about current issues that are bothering you, then you can save a pen in your briefcase for your John or Jane

Be Realistic

Hancock on those divorce papers. You'll soon be singing the Usher song, "Papers"!

Remember to put the big issues that could later affect your marriage out on the table. Don't be pretentious, thinking things will change. That's not the way to go. Don't sugarcoat or push your problems under the rug. They won't simply disappear. Remove the rug, and I bet they'll be staring right back at you.

Are you living in your own reality?

Don't juxtapose your partner's behavior, financial means, and lukewarm love with fantasy just so that you can live another day. You'll be breathing for sure, but not really alive, living. Don't lie to yourself! If he's a drug dealer, don't pretend he's a banker. If he's an abuser, don't pretend he's only too in love. If he's a downer, don't pretend he's merely having another bad day.

Time for a reality check, my friend! The verdict is in: Deal with your reality once you're aware.

Chapter 16

BE FLEXIBLE AND WILLING TO LEARN

IF YOU LOOK around you, you'll notice that whatever the season, the trees and plants had to adapt to survive. They all have their own way of responding to the cycle of life. Animals had to become more creative to get their prey as we became industrialized and more mobile. People had to be sensible in finding ways to mold with the changes of the Universe to sustain life. Call it what you want, survival of the fittest or whatever, but pretty much it means being flexible.

Flexibility allows you to go along with the ebb and flow of life. Here's a refreshing thought: Your relationship, similar to the stages of the human experience, is like the four seasons!

Like spring, when you first meet, you have something beautiful that's blossoming. Life seems so lovely and rosy. It's almost as if you're floating like a dandelion seed head. How exhilarating!

Like summer, as you get to know each other even more, things will heat up if the chemistry is right—heavy dating and emotional attachment to that person. Sometimes, the heat is too much, and the relationship may die off as quickly as it started. For those who can withstand the heat, the relationship continues, like being on vacation on a breathtaking tropical island.

Then you start to analyze the relationship. You've been together for months, and just like fall, the dynamics start to change, maybe to a responsive, majestic, and loving relationship, or else it starts to dwindle and fall off, losing its luster.

And lastly, you're at a point in the relationship when things are calmer and familiar, yet you're being tested to the core and you must figure out how to survive the storms. There may not be much intensity unless you turn on the heat to last another season. Welcome to winter! By now, you're a pro at what to expect from your relationship.

While you're dating, you are in a similar role. You are each a student, experiencing the different phases of each other. You're learning about your lover as well as yourself. You must remove the wool from over your eyes to be ready for life, the chariot of our being. Maybe the person you're dating has an issue that's keeping you from understanding them. So what do you do? Do you keep your firm stance on not wanting to deal with other people's problems or do you adjust, sit them down, and talk about it?

There may be times when your partner wants to get away for a minute. How do you deal with that? A tragedy may occur that changes your partner's view of life, such as the death of a parent, sibling, or a close friend. Are you taking the time to see how this person reacts to these challenges, or do you run?

If you take it all in, you'll see how some of their hardships are a learning curve for you not to make the same mistakes or to find the answer key on how to respond in a similar situation.

I said this to a childhood friend some time ago: Our relationships, especially the intimate ones, are a mirror of ourselves. What we see and experience with this person, most of the time, is originating from us. We are schooling them as much as they are schooling us. Opposites often do attract because they provide the other half of the experience their partner needs.

I was happily surprised a few weeks later when I read something similar to that thought in Christmas Miller's book, *Illuminations: A Road Less Traveled—A Modern Day Seer's Journey of the Human Experience*.

Like the Bended Tree

I've often wondered how my parents managed to stay together after 40-plus years, because they are so different. My mom is one of the kindest women you'll ever meet, but she's fierce when tested. She loves to laugh and to make others feel at home. She always finds a way to bring a smile to my face when she sees me with a stern look. She'll do a silly dance, say something funny, or poke my temple with her index finger. Laughter is her therapy.

On the other hand, my dad is Scrooge reincarnated most of the times. He's serious and doesn't make time for small talk. He seldom laughs, and when he does, it's not for long. Believe me when I say

Be Flexible and Willing to Learn

they have two completely different personalities. Yet, they have found a way to work, once my father came to his senses, or perhaps when my mom realized that she couldn't change him. So the more I think about it, they're two people whose personalities are on different ends of the spectrum. Yet, they balance each other out, each one learning from the other. You can't always be laughing, and you can't always be serious.

An acquaintance of mine expressed to me that you not only need to complement each other but must also be able to match that person's personality when warranted. It means that there may be days when a super goofy girlfriend wants you to be goofy with her. And then there may be times when a business-minded boyfriend wants to take care of business. Will you be ready to shift gears? So to be flexible now is to get ready for the real deal. Once you are in matrimony, the issues that you're quick to judge about other people will start to invade your life.

Allow yourself time to be attentive to each other's needs. Don't be so stuck in your ways that you miss the opportunity to grow. That's what it's all about; growing together and learning from one another. Don't let anyone stop you from keeping your door open to your partner if you know where you're going.

Unfortunately, sometimes when people see that you're happy, they can get jealous and want to sabotage the good thing that you have going on. Yes, I'm even talking about your best friend and those other so-called friends. In some ways, I don't blame the married lady who told me, "Never tell your girlfriends what's going on between you and your man!" I have heard the same for men not to tell on their girlfriends, especially if she's hot and the male friend is not happy with his love life. How many times has this happened, where the listening friend goes after the telling friend's girlfriend or boyfriend?

Of course, we need somebody to talk to, especially when the days get dark, so I would add to that to be cautious when telling your friends all your business.

You must understand that your partner will make mistakes, just like the rest of us. However, when you start spreading yourself too thin, don't hesitate to be honest with yourself and ask if you have done too much to force the relationship to work.

Being flexible is about being open to other options to improve your relationship, now and after you're married. I've heard some people say that they don't like to talk to others about their relationship hardships. Don't confuse talking to a mature adult with letting people lead your personal life. As I've already stated, no other person should be the decision maker of, or too involved in, your daily love affairs. However, caring adults, the ones who have already been down the road, are great mentors who can help guide us to strengthen our bond with our partner.

This is not to say that you want to run to others and tell them all your business so that the whole world is privy to your personal life. But don't be so stubborn to think that after deep reflection, conversations, and all the arguments that you can fix every problem that you encounter with your partner, especially when you feel lost and confused. You can have better clarity when you aren't in self-torment mode. Those are the times when we tend to make irrational decisions.

The beauty in life is that despite what you've been told, you can, and should, come up with a strategy that works for you. If you continue to think your relationship is only about you being happy and there's nothing new for you to learn about your partner, then you're limiting yourself. By the time you decide to pay attention, your partner might have already canceled the wedding.

Remember, flexibility is about allowing yourself to adapt, and learning is about seeing things a new way. What happens to the tree that's not bendable? It snaps when the wind is too strong. Don't let that happen to your relationship.

Chapter 17

SEEK COUNSELING TO RESOLVE PAST ISSUES—CRITICAL!

I CANNOT EMPHASIZE enough how much help counseling can be for people who have serious issues, when the casual conversation simply isn't enough help.

Sadly, I've witnessed people who cannot get off that wagon that is full of misery. And that loaded cart is nothing more than their past issues following them. Some people are able to block some of their childhood miseries. Others choose substance, whether alcohol or drugs, food, or sex addiction. Furthermore, a few pretend that nothing bad ever happened to them. So they live as if they're fine, but is it good if you are still in pain?

I'm a big advocate of getting help before one commits to a partner. There's no workaround for it. Being in a relationship while being eaten up by an internal cyclone is bad news for all.

The person who has these problems will eventually exhibit some of the issues and may be a pain in the ass for no apparent reason. If you're the one in the crossfire, you'll resent, and at times react to, something that's so deep that neither person is aware of what's happening. To save yourself from this dangerously real internal

Seek Counseling to Resolve Past Issues–Critical!

inferno, you must know each other's childhood, adolescent-hood, and current-hood to understand why your lover reacts that way in the present-hood.

A man or woman might lash out when a situation reminds them of their past. You'll be left wondering, "What the heck just happened?" However, by having a tête-à-tête about their past life, you can at least see where they're coming from. I guarantee you, the next time your partner overreacts, especially if it's frequent, then that's your sign.

Remember that humans are reactive beings. Unless you're nagging or you are really the cause of their storm, then that reaction is coming from a past issue that's unresolved. It's like no matter how much you fight for peace there's always that magnet pulling your partner to turmoil. Instead of dealing with this internal conflict, some people will put the blame on you, as if you're the problem, when in fact, they know very well that the problem is in the mirror. You can't have a peaceful, happy, and healthy relationship until you both live in the present.

The more time you spend in the past, whether consciously or subconsciously, the more it is a hindrance from enjoying the present and moving toward a brighter future. I've been there, and it's not a place where you'll want to be.

As you can see, this is serious business that you must manage. Don't wait until you see red. It may be too late to save the relationship. One of the worst feelings is losing your lover when you had many chances to make it work. Nurse yourself before you assign yourself as somebody else's nurse. I only want a healthy nurse to care for me, not one who's sneezing, coughing, and complaining. Who wants that?

Time to Let Go

If you value a fulfilling life, and all that it has to offer, you want your mind, heart, and soul to be as de-clogged and aligned as possible before marriage. It makes a huge difference. Whatever methods you choose to have your issues resolved does not matter as long as they are effective.

If your past has shaped your life unfavorably, or you're plain angry all the time, get help. If you have a substance abuse issue, make sure you go to rehab before marriage. We all know too well the tragedies that befall families because the husband or wife has a substance addiction.

Imagine meeting a woman for the first time, but before you could get her to tell you about herself, you've already picked up the negative vibes. This woman's energy is so dark and suffocating that you would spend time in the Sahara rather than be in her presence. I'm not talking about someone who's trying to ignore you on purpose, but I'm referring to a darkness that's quite different.

When you have past traumas that you're either hiding or don't want to resolve, you still send off those negative signals. You can attract other negative people who feed off that type of energy, or you could meet an agent who is testing your growth. However, if a positive person comes your way, they won't stay long. Positive people don't like to be around negative people for too long.

You don't want to be the negative person that people are avoiding. So take the time to work on your issues. By getting counseling you're helping yourself and your future partner.

Guys Need Counseling Too

Some people, especially guys, think of themselves as weak if they seek counseling, which is, of course, just preposterous. Things happen to both men and women. If anything, guys should be sprinting to get help because they tend to suppress emotional things more than women do. So leave that stigma out the door.

I remember watching a movie where this couple had lost a son who was hit by a car while riding his bike. The dad was incensed, even 16 years later. This man walked around daily like a dark cloud was hovering over his head. His wife's heart filled with sorrow and loneliness and his second son, who was then a senior in high school, barely had a relationship with him. There was always shouting, or no conversation at all.

When his wife went to counseling, she felt much more at peace and relieved from the guilt of what had happened to her son. But her husband refused to get counseling and thought it was a waste of time and money. However, if it weren't for the counseling, this family would continue to suffer from holding onto the guilt and anger of what was out of their immediate control.

So, to all of you out there who need a well-trained ear to help sort out their past, please make it happen. You don't necessarily have to jump out now to go see a psychiatrist, as long as you talk to somebody, anybody, who could help you get past some of your handicaps. But counseling, in whatever way achieved, does that exceptionally well.

Counseling is extremely important for all who are suffering. Sometimes you can counsel yourself by just acknowledging that you could do better. You can stop doing whatever it is that's turning your world into a battleground. But most times, it's not that simple. If you could go see a doctor because you aren't well physically then why can't you visit a counselor when you are mentally off-balance?

It's about healing the heart to make room for a long-lasting and mutually loving relationship. Don't let the past hold you hostage. There's nothing like feeling free of the issues that weighed you down. It's a wonderful, blissful emotion that should be felt by all. Encourage your partner to get help, if necessary. It will save you from great agonies in the future.

Chapter 18

FOR ALL THE GODDESSES OF OUR TIME

I THOUGHT IT was only appropriate that I dedicated a whole chapter to the ladies, and, of course, I didn't forget about the guys, but ladies first. Trust me, it's crucial that you read both sections. Yes, I'm a woman, but I'm not here to side with either gender. I think both males and females have a lot of catching up to do.

We must both acknowledge that the only way that our relationship will survive and thrive is when we both put in collaborative efforts to make it something wonderful.

In order to have a successful union, both men and women must understand certain dynamics of each other's make up.

Ladies, marriage is definitely going to challenge you. Instead of worrying about your maintenance and your goals, you now have to remember that you have a man to consider regarding the majority of what you do.

I know that my independent ladies are the first ones screaming that they have no interest in answering to anyone, but don't forget that without togetherness there is no marriage. No one was forcing you to marry, and you can't escape some of what comes with the package. Thus, if the whole concept of sharing your life is a burden to you then you need to stay single. That's one reason that many people divorce, so if you already know this, then don't walk down that aisle until you see things differently.

The years 2008-2011 should have been penned *the years of the independent ladies* because that's mostly what you heard on the radio and women were quick to show they didn't need anyone telling them what to do. I strongly feel that there's a link between this mindset and divorce as well. We couldn't tune to an R&B station without hearing a song from both male and female singers praising the ladies who could get their own. We were loving it and sang out those songs with a "that's right!" overtone. We would go to the club and the DJ would hype, "Where my independent ladies at?" and we would hear the thundering cheers. After a while, I stopped cheering because even the scandalous women had their hands up in the air. You know, the ones scouting for Mr. Biggs. But sometimes we confuse what it means to be an independent woman.

You can be independent and yet not be absentminded when it comes to involving your partner in your life. Remember that what's important to you will also be important for him to know. See how you enjoy taking care of your hair, getting a mani-pedi, and having that ideal career? Well, that's the same way that you need to take care of your man. I'm not asking you to be anyone's doormat, but you should be observant of your partner's needs just like you are of your own. It won't be easy, especially if you end up with a non-helper who doesn't take care of his end of the equation, but do what you can. In the end, you will know that you did your best and that it wasn't meant to be.

Lonely, I'm So Lonely

Before I tell you anything else, I must talk to those of you who are scared to be alone, without a man. The whole room knows once you show up, Manly is rarely too far behind. It's like a death sentence if you find yourself by your lonely self for even three months. You don't know what to do with yourself. So, after that last relationship ended, without you even knowing why it ended, you suddenly find yourself in another relationship.

Why are you so afraid of being by yourself? Why do you need to be attached to a man every time you turn around? What are you fighting with?

To be alone, especially after a disastrous relationship, is a blessing from the Universe. It's telling you to learn from the last relationship before you move on to the next guy. How can you learn anything about the mistakes made if you don't take time out? The biggest mistake is that you are just setting yourself up to repeat those same mistakes. Again, remember the Penrose's Stairs.

How do you know if you are not the cause of your last relationship ending? But how will you know if you don't stop before saluting the next man in waiting?

Rushing into a new relationship is rarely a good thing. So take your time to work on you, to mend your broken heart, to gain strength, and to be okay by your lonely self, at least for a while.

Spending time alone will help you get in touch with yourself. You'll be surprised at what you find out about yourself. And you will bring some of those great things to the new relationship.

Killing Me Slowly

During the courtship, watch out for all the discussed signs before you marry. For example, avoid the kind of guys who are drama-kings. They will multiply any argument to a gazillion and won't let you have peace.

I've encountered a few of these guys who are ridiculously toxic. Those guys are stuck in a rut and are so used to meeting damaged females that when they meet a woman who knows her worth, they try to bring her to the level of those other females. Some guys might think that you're too highfalutin because you think highly of yourself, but let them keep thinking that.

You can tell a guy is toxic if he isn't at peace with himself and wants a conversation to end in an argument. If instead of being a positive force and contributor to making your life be more productive, he mostly brings sadness, depression, arguments, ignorance, insecurities, anger, and fear, then you are dealing with a toxin. Yep, you need to call the poison control, except the controller on the other line is YOU. You have some decisions to make in a situation like that.

I try to give a "not like the other guy" plea when I date. I'm 100% open and free, mentally, as far as what I want to share with this person. If anything, I find it quite exhilarating because I want to share my life, my experiences, past, present, and future dreams with him. I love to express myself until he gives me reasons to recede. When I see that this guy is secretive, deceptive, and two-faced, I retreat from 100% down to 30% until I am sure I should open my world to this man. Told you Caps are tough! Why should I have to raise another boy who doesn't want to grow up?

This was a harsh awakening for me. Before my ex-husband, I only had one boyfriend, my high school sweetheart of three years. I didn't realize that some men are behind the curve when it comes to truly being and acting like a mature man. Don't consistently give a man the site plan to your heart when he's proven to be less than ready for what you want to develop between you two.

My Unstable Pillar

Before you get married, challenge yourself to open your world to your partner and see how he responds. If he retreats or goes MIA whenever you're in need of emotional, or any kind of support, you may want to slow down a bit.

Support is going to be one of the focal points to the success of your marriage. You must be present for each other! Seriously, marriage is synonymous to many words, and support is one of those unparalleled MUSTS that many couples forget about. All the emotional, financial, spiritual/religious, mental, and familial responsibilities fall under the support umbrella and they're vital.

I ended a relationship partially because of lack of support. That was the last pain that broke my spirit. I had been there for this man through the darker times. I supported him when he needed me, whether it was emotionally or whatever. I accepted him with more baggage than I've ever encountered from a boyfriend. When his friends, work, child, or child's mother would stress and send him to the edge, I was there with open arms to console him and to hear his despairs.

So how come whenever I needed my partner for emotional support in time of great tragedies or any other difficult situations, he was forever a ghost?

He could not come up with a good enough reason why but gave excuses that were confusing and frustrating. Yet he knew who to run to when he needed support. I grew tired of that. When I needed to be rescued, I was all alone, even after having expressed this concern many times.

Why do you have a partner if not to support you through the hard times?

The last time I needed him and he disappeared, my heart went cold and said, "You know what, this man has put you through so much BS, yet you stuck by him. It's your time to wake up and cut the tie because this is not the man for you, darling!"

So, for the first time in a very long time, I listened to that inner voice after adding up all the selfish acts and pains from over the years. As I've said before, I'm still learning and not immune to relationship pains, but like you, I know better.

However, I only had myself to reprimand for this. Even before I got serious with this person, I already knew he wasn't ready. You see, I'm highly intuitive, sensitive, or tuned-in. What some might equate to being an undeveloped oracle. I get immediate signs or sensations about a person. They're not judgments, just warnings. I know the difference because I can notice specific issues, whether recent or from the past, way before a guy tells me anything. I get them for anyone, but only when necessary. So yes, that was the last time that I didn't follow my instincts concerning something so major.

Ladies, your instincts are irreplaceable. The messages are rarely wrong. It's only a matter of time before those signs/warnings become a reality, and for me, that's more often than I can make you believe. So, when I told this ex that he had much to work on before we could take the relationship further, he misunderstood it as being condescending. But here we are today; the warning signs were right once again.

Sometimes, I wish the signs did not hit me so fast when I meet a guy. It can be a downer, but I know it's for the best. Like a protective parent, the Universe is trying to save me from heartaches, but I don't always listen. Still, it's hard to let go when you've been together for years. I trust that the Universe knows why and what it's doing.

It's sad indeed to love a man who doesn't love himself enough to want peace!

Not getting that support now is a way to let you know that you have an unstable pillar in your partner. This is someone who might not be there to help you through the rough moments. Do you want to be in a room all alone, hurting, crying because of a tragedy, while your partner is cruising the streets?

Girlfriend, You're Worth It!

Getting back to you, my sisters, as women, you need to believe in yourselves, including your well-trained intuition, and have confidence of your worth. When people meet you, that self-esteem should speak before you even open your mouth.

I know that people look at me a certain way when I walk into a room because I have a naturally big presence, from the way I walk to my eye contact. I'm not loud, but my composure will announce my presence. I might be clueless about what's going on in the room, but I'm sure of what's going on with me, good or bad. And that's me all day. I am royalty walking a mundane path. Aren't you? See, we only equate royalty with kings and queens, yet, we are kings and queens in our own right. Special in our own unique way. This is not something that I was taught, I was born with that mindset.

But then again, from what I hear, I come from ancestors who were regal, even when they had very little. My father's cousin, the female relatives' protector from male vampires—guys who love to use women—always reminds me of that.

I have doubts about things in life, just like anyone else, but who I AM is not one of them. It took years for me to figure that out. I discover things about myself daily because I allow myself to appreciate and connect with the Universe in a transformative way. I even know that by the time this book is acknowledged by more than just my entourage, I will be more influential, running my own business, or doing something spectacular with my life. I'm not my job. I'm not my friends. I'm not just a lover. I'm more than a mom. Amazingly, when I meet strangers and they take one look at me, I'm as spellbound as they are when they know who I AM by looking into my eyes and by analyzing my composure. I don't allow a guy to mess with my head regarding that for a second, even if I give him time to get it together.

It doesn't mean that you want to strut around as if you're Queen Cleopatra, walking above the clouds and that others are lesser. This simply means that you should see yourself in high-regards, without being condescending or cocky, even if others don't, because you know you are exceptional.

So, if you're battling with low, and sometimes very low, self-esteem, then please stop and build it up now. Look in the mirror and say some positive things to yourself. You may not think that it will affect your marriage, but anything negative can ruin a good thing. You know how a man will fight you for another side chick because she's more sophisticated, successful, glamorous, and adventurous than what he has at home? Well, that's because most men will walk on a woman who isn't self-assured.

Be true to yourself and to where you want to go. After you examine yourself, then it's much easier to see if your partner is compatible with your needs. Sometimes a guy will meet some yet totally suck at the others. But if you've been dating long enough, and you know his strong suits and weaknesses, then you can help him to meet you at your level of satisfaction as long as he's willing to participate. However, that's a decision that you will have to make. Do you have the patience to be a teacher?

Obviously, if you're having to teach your partner how to be a man by continually showing him what he needs to do for you as a woman, then you certainly have your work cut out for you. This is no small feat! There will be much frustration because he will be one step behind, despite what they show in the movies.

This is one of the challenges that women face, especially in this generation. Many of the guys out there, certainly not all, don't know what to do once they're outside the house. They can't carry an engaging conversation when on a date. Some don't even know what to do during a date. You will see that they might start looking around, tapping their fingers on their legs, and smiling sheepishly because they're limited. As stated previously, they might get nervous when you have a strong eye contact. Instead of appreciating the love that you're sharing through sight, he might question what you're looking at!

Check yourself, or else you may end up back peddling just so you could be with that guy who has no goals, no view of progression, and no idea of what it entails to be a good husband. I didn't say great, because, ladies, the great ones are hard to find, but they are around; just look outside of your normal scope sometimes.

You're like a beautiful Nelumbo Nucifera (lotus flower) with several petals that peel away to allow new ones to shine through. That's how your marriage should be: a beautiful, living, and breathing bond between husband and wife. You've heard it said many times that you're a jewel, and that's the truth.

What does it mean to know your worth?

In order to know your worth, you must understand that you are a powerful woman. There's no person superior to you because everyone has weaknesses and problems. It certainly means that you are a goddess who should be about your business. You should allow yourself to experience the different paths necessary for your elevation because of it. The moment you wake, you feel that you have a purpose and are part of a bigger plan.

Ball in Your Court

Again, know that once you walk down that aisle, you're now a part of an equation. Your whole life is going to change, not for the worse, but it should be for the better. One of the interviewees told me that you should be able to continue to do those things that you once did with your friends, even after marriage, and I agree to an extent. But if you're used to being carefree, not concerned about where you wake up, who is rubbing on you at the club, and not being accountable for your actions, I would definitely say to discontinue now if you want to have a healthy relationship with your husband.

Ladies, make it work, if that's what you want, and if you know that you have a good man. A good man could turn into a great husband if he has a great lady standing next to him! Not to sound regular but having and finding a good man is truly a blessing. Can I get a finger snap!

It's true that sometimes you'll be the crème de la crème, but then your man might not know how to appreciate that blessing. He hasn't learned how to reciprocate that love and support or how to say, "Thank you, God, for giving me a woman of so much essence." Since we know such cases exist, don't let that change you from the lovable person that you are. There's a man out there who wants a woman just like you.

Changing yourself for others is never a good idea, unless it's to transform negative attitudes into positive attributes.

We need to do our part and do a better job at home in order to have a more harmonious relationship. Let's stop putting all the relationship struggles on these men. We also need to stop nagging. Be ready to hold your husband's hand, especially when he shows you much love.

When I was married, I didn't play the wife role well. I even knew that I was going to live alone again one day. I saw it in my mind's eye years before my divorce. That's all because I didn't do my homework and ignored the signs along the way before I got married. My poor ex-husband was no better at this either. It was like we were two people who had little, besides our childhood troubles, to connect us as a couple. Many times, I didn't want to be bothered or was mentally in the single mindset. And that made the marriage seem just gray. My ex-husband did what he could until the end when things took a strange turn. Even though my ex-husband was a good guy during our marriage, it just wasn't meant to be.

We went through a dark and painful period after our divorce. I used to wonder how we had changed, but I am now an experienced divorcée who does not feed the chaos. I refuse to go back to that place where I couldn't even feel my own presence. I didn't change myself, or change who I was becoming, to entertain the darkness. If you're already feeling something similar while dating, then take more time to understand your life.

You need to learn as much as possible about your partner. I hope, for your sake, he's a man who is kind, intelligent, sincere, loving, supportive, and mature. How I hope he's mature because there are many boys walking around in grown-men bodies! Those who you don't want to walk with down the aisle. Know that once his immaturity starts to show, you will lose your mind. There will be the start of the breakdown of your relationship, prepping for divorce court. But the ball is in your court from the start. What that ball does heavily depends on you.

No More Illusions!

Go deeper than what you see. Are you exclusively checking out the guys who drive expensive cars? Are you only interviewing the guys who have a Master's or Doctorate degree or own a business? Are you only looking for the guys who make six figures?

We all have preferences, and that's cool, but sometimes we need to go past the exteriors to the person inside. It's great if the guy you fall in love with fits any of the above. However, don't just dismiss a person because he doesn't drive a specific make and model or only makes five figures. He might have more common sense than that boyfriend who had all the above but could not even remember your favorite pastime.

What's more important to you? A man who can support and cherish you, and who would do anything just to bring a smile to your face, or someone who can afford the best but offers nothing else to enrich the relationship? It's not to say that you can't have both, a man that is well off and that can oil your feet but stay flexible.

Heck, what woman would mind having a man who has money and drives a nice car? But his behavior and his natural ability to solve problems, his capability to become an entrepreneur, his passion to enjoy life and have peace is more important to me. Remember that there are some guys driving luxury cars who aren't about much more than looking at themselves in the mirror and who is checking them out. Did you think he was checking you out? Nah, he already knows many ladies fall for the car first.

There are some guys who are driving Benzes and Teslas, yet their salaries don't match their expenses. I know guys who drive those types of cars but make less than $40,000 a year. Don't say I didn't tell you. These luxury cars are like Subways where I live and used to work. But at least I worked in one of the most affluent areas in Atlanta. So try not to be too materialistic because, in the end, those things are just that: *things*.

Again, there's nothing wrong with having standards, likes and dislikes; however, remember that the things that you see don't always align with the person who you barely noticed. You can find yourself a man who has the material gains but then turns out to be your worst mistake. Because after chasing the car, you later find out that this man is so unhappy with all types of problems and countless issues. Don't believe the illusion that what you see always equates with the best.

Your marriage is your marriage! It will reward you with whatever you put into it. It can nourish you, or it can kill you slowly. Get ready for it, ladies. You are the backbone to a happy home. You are strength, so there's not much that you can't accomplish if you want to. You are love, so there's not much that you can't fix. You are the light, so there's not much that you can't understand. You are a precious Jadeite! Be good to yourself, and over time, you will learn how to be even a better wife to your husband.

I Got You, Babe!

A successful marriage will require that you do and understand the following as a wife:

- Love him right—you already know if you're not doing this.
- Look into his eyes once in a while—if he's scared or skirmish when you do this then that's a man who is not comfortable in his own skin.
- Allow him to be a man by not treating him like a second-class citizen.
- Don't think that his world should suddenly be about you and only you, meaning that he can't have any other platonic relationships—TRUST lives here.
- Learn how to make him feel happier through his love language(s).
- Support your man through all rational endeavors.
- Be each other's lover as well as friend—everything else falls under this.

- Have pillow talks—you'll learn a lot.
- You are not his mother and can never be her.
- Give him room to breathe and don't be on his back every second showing your insecurities.
- It is not your job to babysit him, although, sometimes we find ourselves in a position where a man will be so clueless—still, don't baby him.
- Stop playing private detective unnecessarily.
- Show him that he is appreciated, especially if he's showing you that he cares. Again, acknowledge and appreciate him often. This has been a very popular topic in the news lately because apparently, men look very highly at a woman that shows him she's thankful for what he provides—no matter how big or small the contribution.

Ladies, do what you need to do to make your house a home. Remember that you are like Inanna or Oṣun, a goddess of love, of abundance, of fertility, of all that exists. Like those goddesses, you know when to put your warrior shoes away. Carry that torch with pride. Show your man what it means to be a wo-man in grandeur.

Chapter 19

FOR THE EROS OF OUR TIME

WELL, GUYS, IT shouldn't shock you to hear that both you and the ladies need to do chores before marriage. You're just as responsible for the failure or success of your relationship. No, I won't chew you out!

I know many of the good, and the few great, men out there are fed up that they don't get enough props. If you're in that irresistible pool, hopefully, you do get some kind of acknowledgment from your woman. And the ladies, at least the ones who know and understand what they have at home, will surely show you love. I think I've already reminded them of this in the previous customized section, which I'm sure you did not skip. Right, guys?

It's true that in life you will usually hear more about the bad rather than the good, or even the great. Of course, having said all of that, job well done, and I salute you if you are, in fact, a man about your business. You're indeed the true Eros of our time who has graduated from the mass of men who are left behind in preschool, struggling to be responsible and to be good to their women. I love talking to you guys, hearing and seeing how you care for your woman. As if caring for her is like caring for yourself. I love you for that!

On the other hand, you already know if your suit can use a tailor. Instead of you just focusing on you, the time has come to put to work what you were hopefully taught as you grew into manhood. That is, treat your woman with respect and make her proud of having you stand next to her. The way it's expected that she shares her world with you, the same goes for you.

You may not be able to make her happy because that's her job, but you can contribute to her life in a way that makes her happier. When a wife is happier then there's much peace in the house, for we are talkative beings. Showing and giving women the utmost respect and care is not about being antiquated. By the same token, you should expect equal respect from your woman.

Women help make the world go 'round, while some men walk around thinking that they're the Grand Dukes but with very little inkling of their powerful ladies. Any smart man knows this. No, women can't do it alone, but we nurture the world and the life in it. Without our patience, care, and tenderness, God, I don't know what we would have on Earth. Now that you're grown, how quickly you've forgotten!

Every strong man started out forgetting so much, but then his mother's love and bond was the beginning of everything else. That's why a man who lacked this vital potion will often be messed up for a very long time, and sometimes for life. A child could possibly die if not shown that maternal love and sustenance right after birth.

I would concur that there are many women who have been hurt in the past, and they now see men as a dagger. So, unfortunately, you may bear the burden, but that's no reason to settle with a female who is extremely disrespectful and devious. There are plenty such females out there waiting to bat their eyes at their next victim. I have witnessed a few women be totally demeaning to their spouse, and it always bothers me.

I remember one case where this friend had separated from her hubby of 10 years, but they were still hanging out together. She had been the breadwinner, the main decision maker, and the backbone to their marriage. One day, we attended an event and his new girlfriend called his cell. Man! My friend went into a jealous rage for what seemed like an hour. When she dropped me off, I promised myself never to hang out with them at the same time ever again. It was awful!

Guys, set the record straight the moment that a woman wants to show how rude she could be. Let her know that it's unacceptable, especially if her disrespect is for something banal. Of course, this can only be done if you give respect to her too.

Don't be the one pushing your lady's buttons, assuming she's caring and doing right as well, to see how far you could go before the disconnect deepens.

Guys, you must remember that your queen is now your co-anchor. What you do is not only for you, but also for her and your children. For her to be happier is like making yourself happy. Why do you work so hard? You probably wouldn't have to work so hard were it not to take care of your family. You still have the blood of a protector and provider.

Time Is Irreversible: What's Your Plan?

Take the time to learn about what you want in a wife. Should she be a woman who can make you laugh? Are you looking for someone who is hardworking? Maybe a stay-at-home type? Or successful vocationally? Do you want a woman who is patient, caring, understanding, and who loves to be there for you in time of need or whenever? Do you want a female soldier who has experienced life, who knows about the difficulties of the real world, and who knows how to bring peace and resolution in time of chaos?

Now, are you prepared to be the best husband if you indeed meet this incredible woman? Do you cringe at the thought? If so, then you're not ready.

If you want to party hard with the other guys every weekend, hang out all night, and be a playboy, then you have much work to do. I can't think of too many wives who will accept that for long, or at all.

Get yourself together and fix what's broken before you decide to stand at the altar waiting for your bride to come to join you in your misery. Work on yourself before you exchange those vows.

Plenty of guys suffer from anger issues because of work or lack thereof, baby mama drama, family drama, or whatever. If you're one of those guys, take care of your heart now. No wife wants to deal with a man who is plain angry or always temperamental.

It's unattractive to any female is when you forget that you should be a man who can stand on your own. It is not attractive to a female when a man looks like he wants to follow another man around as if he has no brain of his own. Your girlfriend should not feel like she needs to compete with another man. It's already bad enough dealing with the open-gate women out there without having to worry about men too. If you're confused, respectfully leave your girlfriend alone until you figure out what you want. This is not to offend you, but I am finding this to be an issue more often now than ever before.

What's that about anyway? I doubt that you'll have to think hard to get an answer. It's not my job to judge you and your preference, but it causes a lot of pain when you aren't truthful to yourself and your girlfriend. I loathe the term "down-low". I understand that our society is still very discriminatory toward that orientation, but please stop and think twice before you bring a wife and children into that mix. It is very selfish to only think of covering yourself and yet leaving your family exposed to the betrayal and lies. It's not like you don't know what you're doing. You know where you are stepping even before you put your foot down.

Once done, you can't undo the damage. Time is irreplaceable. Please, think twice, guys.

For those of you who only want to make that special lady your gemstone, then listen up carefully. Women can be funny creatures, so you have to take the time to understand your woman. She's unique, unlike any other woman. If you have a confident, self-assured woman then you had better know how to treat her as such, or else you may be looking at moments of frustration later when you aren't meeting her specific needs, whatever they may be.

I know that many guys can be confused when they meet a strong woman who believes in her capabilities and worth. However, there's no need to be scared of these types unless they have a superiority complex.

I remember having a conversation with one of my older male mentors who told me that guys have to alter their attitudes about women of this generation. Since women are doing many of the same things that were once only handled by men, a husband needs to figure out how to keep his lady engaged. She's not going to be satisfied simply with cooking, cleaning, and tending to the children.

Once you've figured yourself out, then it's easier to turn your attention to your lovely lady. A man who's happy with his life will bring less stress into his relationship. Most of the work will come in once you've made a commitment to your woman. She will then look at you as a true partner. Do something nice and unexpected to make her smile often just because of all that she does for you and the children. You know she deserves it.

What are her likes and dislikes? Do you know? You will have to be able to please her in more ways than you did previously. Learn her ways. Does it please her when you help with the house chores? Does she like it when you prepare or start dinner before she gets home? What about massaging her feet, or maybe just surprising her with a little treat?

Marriage can be very stressful if you aren't ready for it. Are you really ready to settle down? Do you have a business plan or a J-O-B to handle your business? How confident are you in yourself as a man? Planning is not only about having financial means either. It's also about your actions and reactions while you're dating. You dine and wine your lovely lady because your plan is to hopefully win her heart so that she could be your wife.

Cherish your courtship time like it's gold!

Continue to expand your horizon. Educate yourself. Learn to love yourself just as a female has to learn the same. If you don't love yourself, stop and don't bring a woman into your life until then.

Soft Skills 101

I have met, heard of, and seen many boy-men out there who can't tell the difference between love and lust, want and need, or true happiness and plain old okay-ism. The ladies talk about you a lot, and there seems to be a delay in how men are responding to the changes that have taken effect since women started to make gains outside the house.

Please learn of what you can bring to a marriage. Learn the ways that you can make yourself irreplaceable in your relationship.

For example, if you marry a professional woman, then money may not be one of her needs, but she will have a need for something, whether it's your time, your touch, your support, or your thoughtfulness. No woman ever has it all in this lifetime. No matter how small the thing that's missing is or how much she walks around as if she doesn't need a man, there is something you can do for her to make her happier.

Believe me, after all the BS from the past, we may try to exclude you from our lives for a while, but eventually, we miss the real deal—your companionship.

It makes a huge difference if she can fall back on you when necessary. This is where you will shine. This is how you'll make her see how much you care. Once you understand that about your woman, providing for her that which she's lacking, then you become a team, lovers, and two become one.

I Got You Too, Babe!

A successful marriage will require that you do and understand the following as a husband:

- Love her right—you already know if you're not doing this.
- Look into her eyes from time to time.
- Do not treat her like a second-class citizen.
- Do not think that her world should suddenly be about you and only you, meaning that she can't have any other

amicable relationships than the one she has with you—Trust Is Paramount Here.
- Know how to make her feel happier through her love language(s).
- Support your woman through all rational endeavors;
- Be each other's lover as well as friend—everything else falls under this.
- Have pillow talks—you'll learn a lot.
- You're not her dad and can never be him. This means that you need to give her room to breathe and not be on her back every second, showing your insecurities.
- Show her that she's appreciated.
- Pay attention to her needs and treat her as an individual.
- Stop playing private detective without a reason.

As you can see, men and women have similar desires, although we pretend we don't. Men want their needs to be met, while women want men to understand their needs. We are progressive beings who enjoy having a man pay attention to us, especially when it's needed most. So, fellas, handle your business!

You already know that a guy can't learn how to be a great husband just from watching who's balling on TV, complaining about how the middleman is not giving him a chance, and blaming everyone but himself for his lack. Your expensive car(s), your clothes, and your money cannot make you a better husband. Yes, you do need them to live a decent life, but you should not be obsessive and addicted to them. Those things could be gone in a *poof*. However, you can be a wonderful man by looking inward and learning how to be happy without depending on others. Shower yourself with self-love. Work on your issues. Know of your life's purpose. Acknowledge that if you constantly mistreat your queen, then you're asking for future misery. Stop running from yourself. The time is now, before you propose.

Guys, if you have found a woman who treats you like a king, who does her best, and you want her to only be yours, then learn how to keep her.

I have seen and known of too many guys whose hearts are forever regretting the fact that they let The One go because they could not handle their business in time. But that's not you, is it?

You're a strong man who knows how to take care of yourself and your partner. You're a grown MAN, not a baby boy. You're the cool dude she fell in love with because you know what it takes to make your relationship work. You don't have to be lectured on how you should handle your responsibilities as a partner. How you should set an example for her to see that her children will have a wonderful father who will teach them great things.

It's a turnoff when a man is overly emotional about everything and cannot logically deal with challenges. Show your wife why she chose you as her husband by keeping as much peace as possible. Do not bring anger every time you walk in the house. Be conscious of how you respond to her, especially at stressful times. Women are very calculative, meaning that if you keep bringing sorrow and screams then trust that she's adding up how often this happens, and one day, she will exit if you don't listen to her concerns. Keri Hilson's song "Breaking Point" describes this perfectly.

Since each woman is different, then you must learn how to be a great husband to your wife by knowing that she has her own ways. Just because she's capable and does not accept nonsense does not make her a control freak. Listen to your woman. Don't be a puppet, but at least hear her out. Pay attention to your household and to what's happening there.

When you look at yourself, you must see a man who is ready to be a husband. Not just any husband, but a wonderful husband! Having a great husband stand next to a great wife makes for a great life and a great relationship!

Chapter 20

EXPANSION OF THE MIND

A GOOD FRIEND of mine recommended the book, *The 5 Love Languages: The Secret to Love That Lasts* by Dr. Gary Chapman. This New York Times Bestseller describes how each one of us has a love language that our partner must nurture for the relationship to last. Dr. Chapman explains, "Love need not evaporate after the wedding, but in order to keep it alive most of us will have to put forth the effort to learn a secondary love language" (2010 20). There are different editions, including ones for women, men, singles, teenage, etc. To sum the key points, when you understand a secondary love language then life can be like a rose. You can smell the sweet aroma of heaven, be in unison, and continue to feel the love.

But when that tending ends or our lover no longer speaks our love language, then we feel like we are no longer satisfied or happy. I immediately knew what he was talking about, but I never referred to it that way. For instance, before I even read the book, I knew that my LL is quality time. I'm protective of my time with my partner when it's supposed to be "our quality time" together. I don't like any unnecessary interruptions except calls for emergencies. If it's not the end of the world, then it can wait.

When I read the book, it made absolute sense to me. The five love languages are: Words of Affirmation, Quality Time, Receiving Gifts, Acts of Service, and Physical Touch. Do you know your lover's language? If you sit down and discuss this, one person might act as if their secondary language is better, stronger, or just plain the best. However, there's no such thing when you really think about it. Why? Well, because we each have our own way of responding to love and what we consider to be the best way to feel loved. It's a matter of preference. Again, some of it has to do with how we were raised, what I call receiving direct love. This is not stated in the book but rather is my own two cents. For instance, if you grew up in a household where your parents used deeds instead of words to show you love, then you might assume that everyone you love responds to such. But that's not necessarily true.

Using actions as a doorway to love is your secondary love language, not your lover's. I'm an apple from that tree. You could be from a home where your parents were very affectionate and said I love you frequently, but then your partner might prefer quality time or gifts. Or if you grew up in a household where your shopaholic mother made the mall her second home and was about buying or spending money, then you might feel like that's the way to show and get love. On the other hand, some people want the total opposite of how they were raised "to prove one's love" but most of us follow the same formula later in life. Or some of us probably did not get any form of direct love from childhood, so we will create our own specific must-have from that lack.

However, I believe that we have more than one love language. Looking at the five love languages, I think a woman wants all five and not just one. We're forever multi-faceted. We want a man who spends quality time with us, showers us with gifts and surprises occasionally, tells us that he loves us, does things that show us that he cares, and of course, knows how and where to touch his lady to make her say, "Let's do it again!"

Don't downplay what your partner prefers. If you stick to your way of showing love without observing, listening, and acknowledging what your partner likes then you're only pleasing yourself. If you're a guy, you'll be calling your boys, questioning what the other guy has that you don't. It's not even about that, but rather, it's about what you're not giving. Anyway, this book is a great supplemental must read for all you lovers out there! Apparently, some of the other people I interviewed knew of this book, but even the ones who haven't read it have wisely incorporated some of the identified ideas in their relationships.

I have also come across a movie titled *The Marriage Chronicles* written, produced, and directed by Paul D. Hannah, which I must also recommend couples to watch together. It was as if the movie was based on my book, yet I had never seen it before. Then again, I was not too surprised because during the interviewing phase of this work, I heard random conversations of what I have discussed here. That's when I knew that I was onto something relevant, that what I'm writing is not exclusively my experience and random thoughts; couples who have been together 12, 20, or 30 plus years are communicating the same thing.

The movie is entertaining, yet it strikes a nerve in the sense that we can relate to what the three couples who went on a marriage retreat are going through. Watch this movie for yourself and take mental notes when the marriage counselor and her husband are having a personal conversation while she's in the bathtub.

Remember how I said that synchronicity always works its magic? Well, the recommended book by Dr. Chapman is also mentioned in the movie. I couldn't believe how what I was learning as I wrote this book was showing up in different ways, as if the signs were also talking to me to let me know that they will reinforce their existence and the fact that they are for real. But they are here, everywhere, as long as you're in a relationship. Now you have two more awesome sources that you can add to your relationship-fixing arsenal.

PART THREE

Chapter 21

AFTER "I DO"

CONGRATULATIONS TO YOU if you've made it this far. Welcome to the new chapter of your life. You've endured the challenges and stayed with me, but my job, and certainly your work, is not done yet. Who said a relationship has an endpoint? There's more to share. If anything, my suggestions until this point are meaningless if you don't keep hard at work. You will notice that some of the details are very similar to what you had to do before your wedding. *Before SEVEN-THIRTY* was preparing you for your wedding. Now, it's going to solely focus on your marriage.

Chapter 22

SO, YOU'RE STILL TALKING?

NOW WE'RE GETTING to the bone marrow of adulthood. This stage of our lives is a lot of fun, yet the most stressful and consuming for some. However, there are ways to calm the madness. This is the middle ground of your life's journey. What happens at this point will determine how the end of your days will be. Meaning, if you spend these years being unhappy, mistreating your partner, not being conscious of how to prepare for the later years then you can expect a miserable old age. Yes, remember Scrooge? That will be you, humbug!

You have made great strides in your childhood and teenage years. Now you have a partner who you've decided to commit to by making it official. Now that you're married, the great things that you enjoyed together while dating should not stop. For whatever reason, many people get caught up and they forget to continue to entertain each other after the wedding. Loosen up and march on in this new journey together.

Two unacquainted individuals, on different roads and coming from different demographics, can only simultaneously end up at the same new hidden place deep in a valley under the ocean if they communicated the location beforehand. Do you see how hard it is to picture that possibility? Well, married life is no different. You must communicate with each other after the big celebration.

You already know some of the things about this person that get under your skin, that you detest, but you should set an environment where communication continues to flourish. I know of some cases where, after a few years in matrimony, couples complain that they don't even talk anymore. You see the husband or the wife come home, dinner is set, but the dialogue is as lifeless as a cadaver. Yet these are the same people who wanted to be together not just 24/7 but rather 25/8—there was never enough time for them during their courtship.

Loss of communication is usually one of the first signs of danger in your relationship. Think about it. Speech is important to us as humans. If that's missing, then the connection will lessen and eventually dissipate altogether. Don't become a victim of that which is in your control. As I stated before, what you talk about is not important as long as there's a dialogue between you and your partner. Now more than ever, share your disappointments, concerns, emotions (good and bad), and of course don't leave out the minutiae of your day. Stay connected. Keep the conversations going!

Chapter 23

BE AT PEACE

THIS IS MY favorite part. If you ask my eldest son what Mommy loves, he will flat out tell you, PEACE. I love having peace in my home and quiet time without the pointless drama. Yes, I love my personal time to calm my always-busy mind. But it doesn't mean that I ignore my partner. I just need me-time to regroup when I have been spread too thin.

I hear of people who want others around them all the time, but since I'm more of an introvert with sporadic extraverted tendencies, I prefer the opposite. However, I cherish sharing my time with my partner. I love to sit down and have dinner together; to watch a movie en deux; to listen to music while leaning my head on my partner; to play games together, or just observe nature. There's power in that bond! Your marriage needs it as often as possible, even if it's once a month.

Many of us feel like the days are getting shorter, or at least it seems that way to me. All the more reason to cherish and make time to be together and reconnect. Just working and coming home then going to sleep after settling in the children is not enough. You have to set and keep an "us" schedule as well. I know that's not always easy because we are so tired after a busy day at work. However, if you help each other with the house chores, you will have more time by the end of the night where you can have at least an hour for just the two of you before you go to sleep. Heck, even think about waking up a little earlier before you have to jump out of bed so that you can give each other a little dose of each other's energy, which should last until you meet again.

Find a trusting person who can watch your child so that you can go out. You both need that occasionally. Don't create a habit of *I can't remember the last time we went out, just the two of us*. Again, I understand that some of us have more family support than others. It's a challenge for a previously single parent, but going out will help you appreciate and enjoy each other again by breaking the monotony.

I remember one couple that made each Friday a date night right in their living room. They would sit next to each other, watch a movie, or just listen to music. I was around 16 when I witnessed this beautiful fondness. The last time that I saw them, at a wedding 16 years later, they were jamming on the dance floor like two youths. The husband was playful and having a jolly old time. It was an incredible sight!

Similarly, I don't have to leave my house to have a good time because I love being in my own space. Whether it's listening to music, reading a book while on the couch with your partner's head against your lap, watching a good movie, or doing a hobby together, there's strength in that unity, in that irreplaceable peaceful time together.

We tend to get so serious after marriage and having children that we bury those days when we used to just chill. In some ways, as you surely can attest, it's not by choice, but we must be aware of the importance of being at peace together. The sooner you do, the better it will be for you and the rest of your household.

If your spouse is the problem, then address whatever issue is at play. Don't let it fester and then wonder why you and your partner are not relating to one another. I prefer to take time out when it's a major issue, but eventually, I will bring it up. I need inner peace, and so I must release.

Clearly, sooner is better than later, but you should do what you must to keep the peace in your house. More time for lovemaking, playing, being at peace, and planning, and less time for drama. Your negative mood can affect your partner's attitude. Make a promise to each other before and after the wedding that you will work together to keep your house from turning into a Ben-Hur stage.

Working on creating a peaceful setting when you're together is worth the reward. The whole point of your marriage is to get to that reward, which is having a fulfilling, satisfying, and healthy relationship with your spouse. There's no way to have that if there's always drama, screaming, door slamming and you're not enjoying each other's company most of the time. Let's keep the peace!

Chapter 24

GROW STRONGER TOGETHER

I HAVE ALWAYS said that I want my husband to be a man with whom I can grow. A man who is a teacher as well as a steward. One of my life themes is knowledge, so I'm mentally captivated by someone who can stimulate my mind. I cannot think of too many people who would say that they want to stay the same and not grow, and after marriage, you should continue to do just that.

The life that you and your partner create is your university.

You must understand, support, and encourage each other to reach for the highest human potential. Once in a while, you might even need to push each other. If your partner has become stagnant, let them know that you see much more they can explore in life.

The Universe is your playground, so don't settle and become so disenfranchised that you end up at the land of the lost. When a man feels lost, he gets consumed by that lack of direction. Most of us want to know the reason we do what we do. We don't want to be hamsters, just turning the wheel.

As husband and wife, know your partner's strengths and weaknesses. Charisse, a woman who has been married for 34 years, advised that it is to know what you're each good and bad at, which creates a balance. You can pick up what your partner lacks and vice versa. For example, if you're good at saving, but your partner is a spendthrift, then you should handle the finances. Similarly, I love a clean house but hate to clean all the time and take out the trash, so if my partner covered that, it would work out so beautifully.

When you learn to work together and teach each other, then you grow into a unit. Can anyone really mess with that? However, if you're selfish and think that the world should serve only you and your ego, then you run the risk of losing it all. Know that you're now one and that their problems will affect you, whether directly or indirectly. The part of you that only thinks about you and not about your partner should be kept in check.

Don't get so delusional to think that you shouldn't have to offer the same of what you ask of your partner. I love to see a successful and loving couple, the type of lovers who work so well together that sometimes words are not even necessary. They work and gel so symbiotically that it's as if they are in their own secret world. In some ways, that's true. But to get there takes time, patience, dedication, commitment, an open eye, and a steadfast heart.

The sooner that you can work with your partner and listen to their aspirations, issues, and concerns, the better and the sooner you will be in synergy.

The goal should be to leave neither one behind. If that does happen, it could create friction between you. You've seen this happen, where the wife gets a promotion and is now the Alpha Wife, or her business is much more successful than her hubby's venture. The guys are often the ones who have a problem with their wives bringing home more money. Some men still have the "I should be the main provider" mentality and there's nothing wrong with that as long as it's not causing problems with your spouse.

Ensure that your spouse is not behind, but rather, right there beside you, looking at you with those adorable and loving eyes, which silently say, "Baby, we made it!" You don't want a great gap where one of you is near the eaves and the other is left on the grade-level.

My parents are the epitome of this. Their love story is one for the big screen. Now in their early sixties, they've been together since their teens. They've worked from very little to now being the golden couple in the eyes of their relatives. It doesn't mean that they have beaucoup money, but they worked together to help each other get to where they could afford a better life for their children and for themselves.

My father often spoke about never wanting to be like the ones who just woke up and wasted the day. He saw more to life than living in lack, so when he and my mom met, they made it their priority to work at getting the life that they envisioned together. Thanks to that hard work and dedication, my four siblings and I didn't experience a hard-knock life. But it all started with them supporting each other and growing together to get to a better place.

Now it's your turn. Take your partner's hand and make it happen. Head to the road of growth together! Your children will thank you for it, and so will your retirement days. If you stop improving, then it would mean that you have stopped living. To live is to grow daily. When two people grow stronger together, that growth is as powerful as a monsoon. Don't forget that.

Chapter 25

LET EACH OTHER BE

SURELY, WE'VE ALL heard that when you marry, you and your spouse are now one. Those who live by the Bible are familiar with verses such as Genesis 2:24, Matthew 19:5, and Mark 10:7 where it states that a man will be one with his wife. This is not a literal statement, but rather, a figurative quote that implies that once married, you and your partner should be in harmony and work toward a common goal. Do not take it to mean that you should forget who you are. Yes, the dynamics of the relationship will evolve as it should, but then remember that two people make that marriage, not just one.

When we start to tip the scale more to one side, then the imbalance will eventually create chaos and is a breeding ground for unhappiness.

Respect each other's contribution to the relationship.

You should take some personal time for yourself. It's as important as date nights and romantic dinners with your spouse. It's like double duty. You must take care of yourself to stay relevant, sane, and in tune as well as make an effort to show your spouse that they are special. But the main thing to focus on here is the fact that you have to let each other be an individual. Let one another breathe when necessary.

It does not mean that you're allowing your spouse to step out on you. You're simply giving your partner room to continue to grow as a person. I'm sure you've heard of guys who feel that their wives just let themselves go. They don't dress sexy anymore. They don't maintain their physical appearance, especially after having children, and they're not as adventurous, etc. The same could be said that some wives have gripes about their husbands not showing them the same respect, not taking them out anymore, or not making them feel appreciated.

The bottom line is that both husbands and wives have a responsibility to keep the fire burning. It's not an easy task, as before marriage or the children, but it makes such a difference.

However, people shouldn't get too complacent, thinking they don't have to try as hard anymore, since they already have their catch. You must understand that if you plan to spend your life with the person you married, then you and that partner will go through a lot of transformations and will evolve as individuals and as a couple. That's inevitable. You have to nurture both, yourself first and then your partner second, but throughout the marriage you must switch between the latter and the former. Don't ignore who you are and close the book on your ambitions, goals, and passion.

Once you're mentally, physically, and spiritually healthy then it will be easier to share yourself with your spouse.

Some might think of this as rubbish, as they say in England, but when you're burned out and exhausted, the last thing that you want to do is set up a nice private dinner for your sweetheart or dress sexy before your spouse gets home. Instead, you'll want alone time to get yourself together. This is why you shouldn't downplay treating yourself so that you'll have the strength to do those nice things for your spouse. And of course, remember to keep a smile on your partner's face as much as possible.

The time that you spend together is golden and so worthwhile that it will reinforce your bond. It's also beneficial for both of you to spend time with your friends, individually and mutually, and go out for a drink. I'm not talking about bar hopping at 2 AM, but just the guys grabbing something to eat, shooting the breeze at the bar, and then going home. Yes, husbands, go back home. Stop heading to those strip clubs while your precious wife waits in bed all alone.

The same rings true for the wives. Get your friends together and go have a good time. Of course, remember your husband is waiting for you. Let your hair down for a few hours and relax. We live in a fast-paced world where new developments can be so yesterday. But to an extent, you control what you do with your time today, as long as you're breathing. Use it in a way that credits your personal nourishment as well as gives you the boost that you need to continue to be the best husband or wife you could be. Relish in the moment you can exhale without worrying about your children and just enjoy the night.

Moja na Mbili means "one and two" in Swahili. That's what you need to remember. One and two merge to create one, not three or Tatu because this is not about the children. Meaning that you're now part of each other for eternity, no matter what, even if the relationship does not last, which we are trying to avoid here. You're forever connected, as your days will now consist of each other and of what needs to be done later when you both get home. It's a beautiful life when you send silent love and smiles to each other from a distance. So make room for love to grow and for each of you to mature as individuals. Once that happens then you will know what it means to be two people who became one in true matrimonial style.

Chapter 26

TRUST: NOT A LIGHT RIDER

WHAT IS THE most important thing to you in a relationship? If I ask 10 people this question, I may get 10 different answers. However, I bet more than half will say this five-letter—no, not four-letter—word.

When I asked my hair stylist this question, she paused for a second. She has been married for 15 years and re-opened my eyes to something very interesting that I too believed. Her answer was TRUST.

Trust is paramount. Without it, there is no HAPPY relationship. Once broken, it's hard to trust again because in the back of your mind there will be that little voice questioning whether this person is lying to you, even when you're being told the truth. I thought about it and was a bit surprised that she did not say love, as I had assumed she would. Yes, I second that most of what you feel in your relationship depend on that five-letter word.

You can open-heartedly love a person with all your might when you believe that this person won't deceive you at the light of a match. You'll be willing to share your deepest thoughts with this person because you know you can trust your partner not to take advantage of your weakness or profound love, assuming that it's genuine. So why risk that?

Well, it's complicated for some. If a guy or a girl didn't have certain experiences in their youth then the urge may surface later, even after marriage. If your spouse has a laissez-faire mindset, it could become even harder to be true if you allow yourself to go in cruise control. Remember when I said that a person would do what they please and stop at their own accord? Well, that's one reason why trust becomes an issue. A person may not have gone through the revolving door of life. A door that will remain in 360° mode until one chooses to exit. Once you start to mess with a person's trust in you, then you might as well have told them to keep the red-alert light on. I don't think that I need to remind you that it takes much work to rebuild it, if it's even possible.

While some people would say love is the most important thing, they forget that trust is intertwined with love. You don't always love someone you trust but should forever trust the person you love, your wonderful husband or wife. If you don't, then you're setting the stage for a catastrophic storm. They're both equally important, but love will relinquish its leading position to trust as the years go by and your relationship matures.

Love, which is kind and not jealous, will stay relevant from a distance. I'm sure you've heard that marriage is not just about love. It will use trust as its eyes and guidance. If you fear that someone will hurt you and abuse your generosity (lack of trust), you will most likely protect yourself when you start to have stronger feelings for that person. This is what most of us associate with love. I was amazed that when I started to interview people who were either married or divorced, trust was spoken of first.

From a woman who has been married for 33 years and dated for five years before marriage: "TRUST is the most important thing." Her advice to young couples: "Follow your instincts. Never listen to the opposite sex or friends telling you about your partner. Realize that's your partner. If you are not willing to work it, then it will not work out."

This is from her husband: "Be true to each other (TRUST). Don't start off lying, so you won't end up lying (TRUST). Always be in touch. Build your foundation together. Communication is key. Always let her know what is going on. You're a team. Whoever is best at an activity, it should be handled by that person. There will be no weakness. Love sometimes has nothing to do with it. Commitment is important."

Here is another story to think about. Keke had a problem with her friend, Jolie, because she felt that Jolie had her eyes on her boyfriend. It was strange to Jolie that she was seen in that light because she had no interest in Keke's boyfriend. Jolie was in her own world trying to find herself. So the friendship dissolved because there was always something in the way of the friendship progressing. Several years later, Jolie discovered that it was Keke's husband that Keke needed to be worried about. He had eyes for Jolie. Keke's husband finally confessed that he had been in love with not just Keke, but also with Jolie, for years. Crazy enough, Jolie had no idea, even back then. When she learned of this revelation, she was shocked because she had never looked at him in an intimate way.

I bring this up because I've seen many females who are ready to fight another female, thinking that she's the problem or the one keeping a husband from doing right. But when you think about it, what is the real issue? Is it your husband, your friend, or yourself that you don't trust?

There was a talk about this on the radio, and many wives called in to say that they trusted their husbands, but it was the single females that they don't trust. Really? The way that I look at it, if you feel secure in your spouse, your husband has proven to be trustworthy, and your relationship is healthy, I don't see what you have to worry about. Your husband has free will. No one can make a grown man fall unless he wants to participate. If some husbands can resist, why can't yours?

People used to ask if I noticed other guys when I was married, and, honest to God, that was the last thing on my mind. I was a humanoid robot at that time, so maybe that kept me from noticing other guys. I thought that if you were trusting, then your spouse was just as trustworthy. But later in life, I have come to realize that's not always the case. During my separation, while still quite vulnerable and not having a care in the world, I cajoled myself to listen to my wild-side. That's when I realized that a man or a woman will do whatever they want if they so choose.

I had a new friend who meant a lot to me, and I wanted to help her because she was going through hell and back. At least that's the best way that I could explain what was happening to her. There was always something not going right. She and I connected instantly when we first met, and it was nice to have a new friend. But months later, something strange started happening. Somehow her hubby went through her phone, got my number, and sent me a message. That was very unexpected and puzzling. Since it was almost my friend's birthday, I thought he was trying to surprise her and needed my help, so I called him to see what was going on, what he needed to talk to me about.

I should not have been that astonished, but I was! To my surprise, the philanderer had no such thing in mind. He started telling me his business and I had no idea why. Anyhow, I explicitly told him the only reason why I had returned his call was that I thought he was trying to do something nice for his wife and needed my help.

So, I thought he had gotten the message not to call me again because it wasn't appropriate, especially since he was not handling his business at home. Plus, his wife was a sweet and caring person who just needed a boost of confidence and self-worth. But then something was just not feeling right after that. What made me put up a stop sign in this drama was when he saw me while he was with his wife and he acted strange, as if he couldn't speak to me. However, he had the nerve to text me the next day to find out how I was doing. Why couldn't he ask me that when he saw me the day before? Why was he texting me?

The whole scheme did not sit well with me at all. He even went out of his way to acknowledge me when he barely had time for his wife. One past experience in particular had taught me to be more alert and not to allow myself to fall into another trap. Both my father and my then-boyfriend exclaimed, "Don't be naïve!"

Yet, his dearly devoted wife was plain clueless as to what this man was up to. I already knew about her issues, about how he made her feel, and how she felt about herself and her marriage. So, I quietly exited because I wasn't trying to be in the middle of this confusion. To this day, she does not know why I pulled the disappearing act. I didn't know what to do. I could have told her, but she was hurting and believed him, even when he was telling her tales that would make any loving and supportive woman pull the ENOUGH card. I didn't want to be that friend who caused a greater schism between them because she was already comparing herself to other females. It wasn't her, it wasn't me; it was her dissatisfied husband. I'm not talking to you if you're not caring for and supporting your husband. This friend was one of those rare wives who was a sweetheart and she didn't deserve that.

I had another case where I had met a man and his wife while in line to vote. We stood there for more than four hours, so a few of us started to talk and exchanged information. Now, sometime later, the lady's husband called and said he was working in another state, and we kept in touch for a few weeks until I realized that this man had something else in mind. I was trying to meet new people, since I had just moved from Maryland, but he was trying to swing. Yet he made it sound like his relationship with his wife was good. Really? I fell for this confusion once but never again. I saw where this was headed, and I deleted his number from my phone.

By then, experience had taught me to remove myself from such situations, as people always look for a time of vulnerability to get under your skin. I didn't know what his situation was with his wife, nor did I care. Some things are not meant to be repeated in one lifetime. What did I tell you? Life is nothing more than a shipload of affable and ghastly experiences. Hopefully, you learn quickly to reduce the bad ones.

It does happen that you could have a wonderful and loving spouse that would go to the end of the seas and back for you, and yet you might take it all for granted. What I've learned in these situations is that people will do whatever they want to do, regardless of how their wives or husbands perceive that they should be. If your partner wants to have a love interest on the side, you can't stop them. If this person wants to be with you and only you, that's already decided without you forcing it.

Some of you might be saying, "Not my partner!" but yes, even your partner. Sometimes it's just karma doing a little ass kicking. You know, like maybe while dating, you cheated on him and although he said he forgave you, there's a part of him that will forever hold onto the fact that you betrayed him. Or you treated her badly and so she seeks appreciation somewhere else. Some men and women have communicated that they can't be with just one partner, even after matrimony.

This is why it's critical that you get to know about your partner and pay attention to the signs of commitment, or lack thereof. You don't want to be deceiving or secretive just because your spouse is loose. This is not just for the guys.

If you don't have confidence that your partner is telling you more truths than lies, then what's the point? So, ladies and gentlemen, building that trust should have started while you were dating and should increase throughout your marriage. If it was not there while you were dating, it will not be there after your wedding day. Trust is what keeps you sleeping well at night, no matter where your husband/wife is. Trust is the backbone to all doubts or rumors from jealous friends. Trust is key to knowing that your relationship will grow into something beautiful and divine. So don't play with it.

I did not think that humans could fall so easily, but we do; however, we do so mostly when we are unhappy at home or our spouse is pushing us away. If you want to avoid unnecessary chaos, then start on the right foot and take care of your spouse so that they won't use the lack as an excuse to walk into the wrong room. Your life will be quite cumbersome if you constantly have to question what your spouse is doing or who is on the other end of the line.

Marriage and trust go hand in hand. So again, do not take trust lightly. It's the backbone to building a great relationship with your partner. Now that you're married, trust will be more important than ever. If you find that you cannot trust your partner at some point in your marriage, you need to lay the cards on the table and talk about what has happened to erode that trust. Is it him? Is it you? Be frank about what exists.

If others are telling you tales about your spouse, don't let your emotions run wild to condemn your partner. Do your own investigation to find out what is going on and why. I have observed spouses who don't care much about trust anymore because it's been tested too many times, yet they remain married. You don't want that to be you because these people don't live as, or enjoy each other, the way a married couple should. It's like Pi and the Bengal tiger on an open sea!

Hopefully, trust is not one of those things that you're questioning in your relationship. It's so vital to a healthy relationship that it would be like being deep inside Linville Caverns—total darkness if it does not exist in your life. The happiness of your marriage depends on it.

Chapter 27

CREATE YOUR OWN FOOTSTEPS

IF SOMEONE ASKED you today what your ideal married life looks like, how would you respond? If that's not the life that you're living or working toward, then do what you need to do to get there. We often find ourselves so bombarded with the unnecessary blockage that we forget that the things in our lives were brought in by us.

Did you take a mental walk around the Tree of Forgetfulness?

Stop for a second and think. Did anyone hold a gun to your head to force you to marry your husband or your wife? Did you choose your friends? Did you pick your career? So you see, if you're married and are unhappy, then somewhere along the line, you stopped creating the life that you wanted by accepting less or by being too oblivious. It's not always easy to cleanse your environment, but it will make your life a lot simpler and happier when you do.

As a newlywed, you must be conscious of how you want your life to be. When you are, then chaos will make way for order. You won't be immune from life's perils, but you'll definitely be a lot calmer. You'll take responsibility for what isn't working anymore and how to resolve it. You and your spouse will be on common ground since you both have a duty to create a life that's mutually acceptable.

Don't live someone else's life. Now, ask yourself the same question. Is this the life that you want?

Make a list of what's not working well right now, share it with your partner, and talk about that list. Actually, you both should make a list and discuss it. Observe whether or not some of the issues are similar. Peace is important in my life, so when I start to feel like my world is falling apart, you had better believe I express that. Especially if the chaos is not coming from my end. I like to evaluate what is going on around me and make the necessary amendments.

I'm accountable for what affects me, so I make it my job to stay on the alert when I start to feel lethargic, uninspired, frustrated, or just plain unhappy. I only notice this because I want to create the life that I want, and not live a life that will give me high blood pressure tomorrow.

Do things together. Enjoy each other's company. Talk things out. Play together. Agree to disagree. Trust each other. Support each other. Make changes when necessary.

At least then you cannot blame anyone else for your unhappiness. The more I think about it, the more I seriously believe that although marriage can be hard work, it's not hard in itself. It's our stubbornness and lack of attention to our relationships that make it appear so. If we had taken the time to know ourselves, know our boundaries, be realistic, be flexible, be willing to learn about each other, and get counseling to be whole, then we would be ahead of the curveballs thrown in our paths.

When we still have so much work to do before marriage and ignore the signs, we pay with the sacrifice of our happiness after marriage. But the power is in your control. Don't let the dismal signs dictate the direction of your relationship. Capture the signs as they arise and put them in perspective. Your happiness is at stake if you don't.

According to the article, "Five Things Good Partners Say to Each Other," 40-plus-year clinical psychologist and marriage counselor, Randi Gunther, Ph.D. compiled the following list:

- We're in this together.
- You're better at this than I am.
- I'm angry.
- Please tell me what's going on.
- And then finally, say things face-to-face.

"Couples who are actually there for each other, physically and emotionally, are much closer" (2012).

As you can see, this list supports what I've already expressed in this book.

It's safe to say that marriage will continue to be a part of our adulthood. Yet divorce might not be too far behind. However, since we now know that there are signs that help guide the state of our relationship, for better or worse, we can bridge the gap or break off the divorce link from following your every move before you say *I do*.

It's serious business to pay attention to the signs while dating. It's critical that you understand and know those signs. But more so, it's a matter of greater importance to take action, to respect and be realistic about what you discover. And lastly, make your marriage be as heavenly as it was meant to be after working through the signs. Do your best to keep the feeling that you experienced when you had that first husband-and-wife dance. Remember how happy you were as you felt each other's heartbeat like the beat of the beautiful song that you chose. Go back to that moment as often as you need to. The future is yours to shape. You already know the remedy to save your marriage and stop the symptoms *Before SEVEN-THIRTY*.

WORKS CITED

Cates, Gilbert, director. *I Never Sang for My Father*. Janel Productions, Columbia Pictures Corporation, 1970.

Chapman, Gary. *The 5 Love Languages: The Secret to Love That Lasts*. Northfield Press, 2010.

Coontz, Stephanie. *Marriage, a History: From Obedience to Intimacy, or How Love Conquered Marriage*. Viking Press, Penguin Group Inc., 2005, p. 125-129.

"5 Things Good Partners Say to Each Other." *MSN Living*, Hearst Communications, 16 Feb. 2012, www.living.msn.com/love-relationships/love-sex/5-things-good-partners-say-to-each-other-1 [Accessed 01 July 2012].

GSMA Intelligence. "Definitive Data and Analysis for the Mobile Industry." *GSMA Intelligence*, 16 Aug. 2018, www.gsmaintelligence.com [Accessed 16 August 2018].

Works Cited

Linn, Allison. "Sometimes We Cheat on Our Partners about Money, Survey Shows." *TODAY.com*, TODAY, 24 Apr. 2012, 7:22 AM EDT, www.today.com/money/sometimes-we-cheat-our-partners-about-money-survey-shows-731779 [Accessed 21 Aug. 2012].

"Marriage." The American Heritage Dictionary of the English Language, Edited by Edited by Pickett, Joseph P. and Steven R. Kleinedler, 5th ed., Houghton Mifflin Harcourt, 2012, p. 1076.

"Marriage." *Merriam-Webster.com.* Merriam-Webster, 2012 [Accessed 12 July 2012].

"Matrimony." The American Heritage Dictionary of the English Language, Edited by Pickett, Joseph P. and Steven R. Kleinedler, 5th ed., Houghton Mifflin Harcourt, 2016, p. 1084.

"National Center for HIV/AIDS, Viral Hepatitis, STD, and TB Prevention." *Centers for Disease Control and Prevention,*

Centers for Disease Control and Prevention, 18 June 2018, www.cdc.gov/nchhstp/dear_colleague/2018/dcl-061418-YRBS.html [Accessed 12 Oct. 2018].

O'Callaghan, Sean. *The Compact Guide to World Religions*. A Lion Book, Trafalgar Square Publishing, 2010.

Serling, Rod. "Where Is Everybody?" *The Twilight Zone*, season 1, episode 1, Cayuga Productions, CBS Television Network, 2 Oct. 1959.

Scorsese, Martin, director. *The Aviator*. Miramax Films, 2004.

Talbert, David E, director. *What My Husband Doesn't Know*. Image Entertainment, 2012.

Vasel, Kathryn. "Cost of Raising a Child: $233,610." *CNNMoney*, Cable News Network, 9 January 2017: 11:01 AM ET, www.money.cnn.com/2017/01/09/pf/cost-of-raising-a-child-2015/index.html [Accessed 15 Aug. 2018].

Wagner, Peter, and Wendy Sawyer. "Mass Incarceration: The Whole Pie 2018." *States of Incarceration: The Global Context 2016*

Works Cited

| *Prison Policy Initiative*, 14 Mar. 2018, www.prisonpolicy.org/reports/pie2018.html [Accessed 12 Oct. 2018].

Wikipedia contributors. "Marriage." *Wikipedia, The Free Encyclopedia*. Wikipedia, The Free Encyclopedia, 01 July 2012 [Accessed 01 July 2012].

FINA ORIA [née Finerve Louis] is from Marchand-Dessalines, Haiti, by way of West Orange, New Jersey. She is Fina in reverence of her beloved paternal grandmother, Afine!

Fina has a Bachelor's degree in Computer Science and a minor in Business Law & Public Policies from UMUC. She is a Licensed Commercial Real Estate professional, a Certified Aromatherapist, and an adventurer who loves to learn new things and meet new people.

As a natural intuitive and a problem-solver, Fina has been the go-to person for many men and women who needed a boost of self-confidence and ways to empower themselves. She is living up to the name Fina, which means messenger. Since her divorce, Fina has been sharing her experiences, relationship insights, and wisdom with others. She writes to help both men and women from repeating the same mistakes and enabling an unhealthy relationship with someone who is unworthy of their time.

She loves to read, listen to music, dance, travel, and learn about other cultures.

Fina Oria is the proud mother of three young kings.

For more information on her work:

Visit Fina Oria's website: www.before730.com

Follow her on Twitter: @Before730

Instagram: @DecodeLifeBefore730

Facebook: /before730

Subscribe on YouTube: Decode Life Before 730

For speaking engagements: WorkWithFina@before730.com

www.ingramcontent.com/pod-product-compliance
Lightning Source LLC
Chambersburg PA
CBHW071957070526
44583CB00015B/1229